Do's and Don'ts
for
Ancestor-Hunters

Angus Baxter's

Do's
and
Don'ts
for
Ancestor-Hunters

Genealogical Publishing Co., Inc.

Library of Congress Catalogue Card Number 88-82012
International Standard Book Number 0-8063-1227-0
Made in the United States of America

Cover photograph by Nan Baxter

Contents

For Nan, my wife, who has
honored me with her love
for forty-five years.

O my Luv is like a red, red, rose,
  That's newly sprung in June;
O my Luv is like the melodie
  That's sweetly play'd in tune.

As fair art thou, my bonnie lass,
  So deep in luve am I;
And I will luve thee still, my dear,
  Till a' the seas gang dry:

Till a' the seas gang dry, my dear,
  And the rocks melt wi' the sun;
And I will luve thee still, my dear,
  While the sands o' life shall run.

Robert Burns

Call back yesterday — bid time return

(William Shakespeare — Richard II. Act III)

Introduction

his book is designed to help three kinds of people, and, perhaps, make them laugh a little and learn a little:

(1) Those who have never even thought about tracing their ancestors
(2) Those who have just started on the magic journey
(3) Those who have been tracing back for years and have reached a dead-end

Ancestor-hunting (or genealogy, call it what you will) is not an exact science. True, there are formulas or equations in the form of certain essential records to be searched, and the right order of so doing (from YOU backwards, and not from a famous person who shares your name down to you!), but a large part of the search is controlled and directed by vivid imagination, flights of fancy, an ability to let the mind flow freely, an adaptability to new methods and new ideas, and, of course, infinite patience and determination.

The regular, stereotyped avenues of research are the areas where there is the greatest chance of success and the greatest possibility of failure—because of obstacles created by the ancestor-hunter unassisted by anyone else. These are the areas where the big mistakes are made, where rigidity of thought is a vice and the ability to set the mind in flight is a virtue. These

1

mistakes are made equally by the expert and the beginner. Remember that "Today's beginners are tomorrow's experts" is a reversible slogan.

You may be saying at this point—if you are at all interested —"Oh, I could never trace my ancestors; I don't know any- thing about my family." This is not true. We nearly all of us know something, but if you don't, this book will tell you where to look to find out.

Few people could have been as "cold" as I was when I started. My father had died when I was four, and I only knew the places of his birth and death. I knew absolutely nothing else. I had no living grandparents, an uncle who knew noth- ing, and a mother who was not co-operative. After making all sorts of stupid mistakes (I had no books to guide me) I even- tually traced my family back for 500 years. If I could do it, then so can you. The records are there and I will try and help you find them.

How far back will you get? How much will it cost? No one can answer these questions with certainty, because so much depends on you and your will to succeed and on the conditions and availability of the records you will need in your search. You should be able to trace back for at least 200 years, and it should not cost you more than $200, spread over a couple of years, to trace one side of your family.

I hope this book will persuade you to start the great journey, will help you on the way, and ensure you reach your destination more easily. It does not set out in detail every possible source of genealogical information—there are other books for this—but it will prevent you from creating your own dead-ends.

In forty years of tracing my ancestors and helping people trace theirs, I have made my share of mistakes, heard lots of funny stories, had many adventures, and quickly discovered that ancestor-hunting is fun—and all reports to the contrary, fun is what life is all about!

ANGUS BAXTER

1 • Why Start at All?

Why on earth would anyone want to trace their ancestors? Why bother about the dead past when there is the exciting present and the unknown future? Do you think you'll find "blue blood" in the family? Or a missing fortune? Or even an unclaimed title? Do you imagine yourself as a grandee of Spain, or a Scots laird with 10,000 acres of heather?

A number of earnest young sociologists and psychiatrists have told me we are searching for our roots because we live in a changing society constantly on the move. They told me we have a desperate need for stability in our lives. Perhaps they mean we are all "yuppies" with a yen for yesterday!

My wife and I have traced our families (or at least one side of each of them) back nearly 1,000 years, and we don't feel any more stable than we did when we started! I think we—and you—are pretty stable to begin with, anyway.

What then is the reason for this extraordinary interest in searching for our roots? An interest which has made tracing ancestors the most popular hobby in the world! I think that the explanation is very simple and straightforward—we all of us have a love for our family and a natural curiosity about our origins.

Some of us have never tried to trace back because we thought it was impossible, or too difficult, or too expensive, or too time-consuming. It is none of these things. It is possible for almost everyone. It is not easy, but all obstacles can be overcome; it is not expensive because it is a pay-as-you-go hobby and you can stop and start as you please. It will take time, but YOU decide how much time you can spare, and YOUR time is YOUR own to give. If you have just retired or are about to do so, ancestor-hunting can be the most time-filling work in the world. If you are younger, with a busy working day and all the stress of earning a living, there is nothing more relaxing than an evening spent in your own home tracing your forbears.

If you want to leave a legacy to your children or grand-children, what could be better than to give them a past as well as a future? If your hobbies are golf or gardening, then in the winter you can forget missing a putt or fighting the crab grass, and search for your roots instead.

If you are descended from the early settlers of our country you can go down in local history as a chronicler of the past by tracing your pioneer forbears and writing the story of them for the local archives or library.

OR, if you just want to have fun for no particular reason at all, then read on—ancestor-hunting is for you!

Your eventual rewards will not be financial; they will be much more valuable—the stuff of romance, the magic of the journey you have made back through time. You will not only know the names of your ancestors for many generations but you will find out what they did, the kind of house they lived in, the wages they were paid, their ages when they died, and, quite often, the cause of their death. Your own research into the by-ways of social history will tell you about the clothes they wore, the food and drink they consumed, and, perhaps, the part they played in the life of the area in which they lived. If they emigrated to another country from the land of their birth you will find out the reason why they left hearth and home and the bosom of their family to sail the seas to a strange and often hostile land. Was it religious persecution? Eviction by a cruel landowner? Poverty? The spirit of adventure? The information is waiting there for you to discover.

Your ancestors will become living, loving people of close acquaintance, and one day, quite suddenly, some incident may trigger a deep, emotional feeling of kinship with those members of your family who preceded you on this small planet. You will realize that the word "family" encompasses many hundreds of people over the past centuries whose blood you share, however diluted it has become with the passing of the years. You will feel close to the hitherto unknown men and women who helped to form your character and your physical appearance.

All you need to start on your life's most romantic journey is love and determination and patience.

So you decide you will try and trace your ancestors. What rewards will you receive? Nothing tangible, nothing that you can clean and polish and place on display. You will find no missing fortune and no unclaimed title. (Alas, for dreams!) You may not even be applauded by your own family. In fact, some members may actively oppose your research—afraid, for hidden reasons of their own, that you may open a closet door on some family skeleton! We will talk about these fears later on. For the present, we will concentrate on getting you started.

2 • How Do You Start?

This is simple and easy to decide. You start with YOU and nobody else. You do NOT start with someone famous with the same surname as you—someone who lived a long time ago. You start with you yourself and you work back through the years. There is no other way, no short-cuts, no guesses, no assumptions.

First, you must decide which side of your family is of the greatest interest to you. I think the majority of us decide on our father's side because we share the same surname, but there is no hard-and-fast rule about this, and the choice is yours. Perhaps you know much more about your mother's family than you do about your father's side, and that may be a good reason to start on the maternal side first. On the other hand, you may be closer to relations on the paternal side and find them handier to consult.

In my own case, my father died when I was only four years old, and I was brought up amid my mother's eight surviving brothers and sisters and their countless offspring. So what was my choice? Quite obvious, you will say, you started on your mother's family. Wrong. I was intrigued by my complete lack of knowledge about my father's background and by the fact that when, as a child, I asked my mother about the Baxters I was always told, "Oh, don't bother about them—they were no good

6

except for your poor, dear father." In addition, with a few exceptions, my mother's family seemed to me to be a cold, unloving family, always bickering among themselves. So my search for my roots at that time was to concentrate on the Baxters.

As you see, there are several different factors which will affect your decision. Of course, we are only talking about the one side of your family you will start with. As time goes by, and as you serve your apprenticeship in the craft of genealogy, you will eventually be tracing your ancestors on both sides, and later you will expand your search still further into other branches.

It is wiser to concentrate on one side of your family at a time, otherwise you will only become confused with the dozens of names you will collect as time goes by. Was that Ernest Thompson or Ernest Thomas? Was it Ann Williams who came from Cardiff or Ann Richardson? You will also find when you are checking long lists of names in church registers or census returns that it will be much easier to look for one surname than four or five. Of course, if two or more sides of your family came from the same city or village, that is quite a different story— you will save time and money by looking for them all simultaneously.

As you talk to members of your family you will hear mention of other branches, of distant cousins, or connections by marriage. Be sure you write it all down, but concentrate on the one side on which you started, and set the miscellaneous names to one side for use in the future when their turn comes.

Your search will never end unless you decide to work on two sides of the family and then stop. However, ancestor-hunting is an incurable addiction, and you may not be able to take the "cold turkey" cure!

So let us talk now about the actual start of your search. What do you need in the way of tools? Simply a 3-ring binder, a small notebook, a ruler, and a ballpoint, plus three or four large sheets of white paper (about 30″ x 24″) which you can buy quite cheaply in any art or stationery store.

The first thing you will be doing is to write down all the information YOU have about the family. You must be very careful to distinguish in your notes between what you know is a FACT and what you believe to be true. A fact is something supported by evidence. Your own date and place of birth is a fact if you have a copy of your birth certificate to prove it. It is not a fact if you only know what your parents have told you is your date and place of birth. Perhaps they have made a mistake. Who knows? It is unlikely to have happened in your case, nor is it important, but once you are another generation back, if you make any assumptions at all, you may have created a complete dead-end for yourself. So you must learn to always distinguish between FACT and BELIEF. If you have no documentary proof of an event, then in your notes write beside it "according to Aunt Mabel" or "according to tombstone." Yes, even the dates given on a tombstone may not be correct! If you do have documentary proof, then write "according to birth certificate"— or whatever the documentary proof is.

Now you are all set to start with YOU, and this is when you start talking to everyone and collecting family stories, and this is where your troubles will really begin because you are dealing in the main with memory, and memory can play tricks. Let us talk about this in the next chapter.

3 • The Start

In many ways, the actual start of the search is the most diffi-cult thing you will encounter. It is the basis for all your work, and the possibilities of making a mistake are very great. If, of course, the original immigrant in your family is still alive you will have practically no problems, but the chances are that it was your grandfather or great-grandfather who came from the "old country"— or the original immigrant may have been even further back. However, as we go along I will try and cover all angles.

At this point you should sit down and make a list of all the people you need to talk with or write to. Make sure you cover EVERY member of your family. This is vital because just one member of your family may possess information which no one else has. After you have written down the names of your imme-diate relatives still living—your mother and father, grand-parents, aunts and uncles (and their children)—add the names of any old family friends you know about. Maybe your grand-father, before he died, told an old friend all about his life in the old country before he emigrated—information he never both-ered to pass on to anyone else.

Let me tell you a story to illustrate the kind of thing that can happen. When my wife and I started to trace her Pearson ancestors we knew they were Scots from way back. My wife was born in Scotland, as were at least five generations back—to her certain knowledge. She did remember that when she was a small child her grandfather told her that the family had come from England some two centuries ago. Years later, after grandfather had died, she mentioned his remark to her father. He told her she must have misunderstood: "The Pearsons have always been Scots—there's not a drop of English blood in our veins!" You have to understand that in Scotland if you are partly English you keep quiet about it!

In due course, as we worked back over the years we reached an ancestor who had been married in a particular place, fathered children there, and died there—BUT he had not been born there. We searched records for fifty miles in all directions without finding any trace of his birth. We were at a dead-end. Then we realized that the date of his marriage was a little over 200 years before my wife's conversation with her grandfather. This must have been the man who came from England! This was why we could not trace his birth. This set us off in a totally different direction, and eventually we found his birth in England. There is much more to this story which I will tell you later on, but this brief account is simply to make clear the point I made above—that one person may have information not given to anyone else. My wife's grandfather had never told his sons and daughters about the English connection, and without his remark and my wife's memory of it, we would never have been able to trace the family back.

You may be lucky and find that a cousin has already been "bitten by the bug" and has traced the family back. Be very grateful, but quietly check the accuracy of his or her research. Strange things can happen—people can make mistakes, or they can assume a family relationship which is actually incorrect. There can even be cases of deliberate deception. Many years ago, as the result of a radio interview, a listener got in touch with me and asked for my help. In those days I was not fully occupied with writing and lecturing, as I am now, so I was quite willing to assist her in solving her problem. On the surface it was quite simple. She was descended from the famous Dr. Samuel Johnson, the eighteenth-century English wit, author, and lexicographer. An aunt of hers had worked for some years on the family tree but she, herself, wanted to find out if she had any Johnson cousins and had come up against a brick wall in her research. I went to see her and, because she was a nice woman and I had time to spare, I told her I would check a few things out for her. She gave me a very detailed copy of the family tree, complete with all information of births, marriages, and deaths back to the famous Samuel. I made a few enquiries and soon found that the whole tree seemed a little odd. I then checked the vital events recorded by her aunt and found that the entire family tree was fictitious—none of the events recorded had ever taken place—and to top it all I found that Dr. Johnson had never had any descendants! The aunt, anxious to claim descent from a famous man with the same surname, had painstakingly concocted a family tree out of her own mind. I have never come across another case like this, but you never know—so always check, check, check.

A little later we will talk about the basic records which will give you information about your ancestors—civil registration of births, marriages, and deaths, church registers, census returns, and wills—but for the moment let us continue to talk about your own family.

I mentioned earlier that you must be prepared for your relatives to take little interest in your search and, in some cases, to oppose it actively. As far as the first people are concerned you will just have to grin and bear it. Not everyone is interested in tracing their family back. At times you will find that ancestor-hunting is like plowing a very lonely furrow. Your problems will lie with the second category because these are often the people with the most knowledge. Perhaps they are aware of a skeleton in the family closet, or afraid you will discover it yourself. Maybe they are afraid you will find—horror of horrors!—that great-grandfather was born out of wedlock. Who cares about that sort of thing? I don't, and I surely hope you don't either. You must use all your charm and tact to persuade them that it is very unlikely you will find anything out about the family which would make them unhappy, and, even if you do, it will always remain a deep, dark secret known only to you. Perhaps they are afraid you will find out that grandfather was the black sheep of the family. Explain that it is almost impossible to find out anything about the character of your ancestors unless they have been written up in local history books or, perhaps, a church magazine.

In all my own ancestor-hunting I only discovered one bit of information about the personality of one person, and that was my grandfather. I never even met him because he died when I was five years old, and he lived far away. In the very early days of my searching I found someone who told me of a very old man—he was over ninety—who had been a friend of my grandfather's. Of course I went to see him. I said, "I believe you knew my grandfather." He replied, "I've known a lot of people, and they're all dead. What was his name?" "William Baxter," I replied. He furrowed his brow, looked into the distance and said, "William Baxter? William Baxter?"— and silence fell, until suddenly he cried out, "I remember! I remember! That was Whiskey Willie!" I was thrilled. My grandfather had ceased to be just two names on a death certificate and had become a living human being with a taste for whiskey!

If you have an elderly aunt or great aunt, this may be like striking the mother-lode. Women are the custodians of family history—they know when and where people were born, who married whom and, in some cases, who *had* to marry whom! They know when people died and the cause of death. Remember, too, that they can tell you not only about the events of their own lives, but also about the events they heard of from their grandparents. In the clear mind of an elderly person you may find 150 years of family history—a rich source of material just waiting to be uncovered.

I remember many years ago, when my mother-in-law was over ninety, she expressed a wish to visit the area of Scotland from whence her Grieve ancestors came—the valley of the River Nith, near Dumfries. We spent a day wandering round looking at old farmhouses once owned by her ancestors and visiting old churches and churchyards. When we were walking round among the graves in one of these she suddenly stopped and looked at a tombstone. "Helen Grieve," she read out. "Born 1830. Died 1838. I know all about her. She was a lovely child with long, golden hair. Everyone loved her, she had a beautiful disposition. She had consumption, though, and when she was just eight years old she died—a day after her birthday." I said to her, "Margaret, all that happened fifty years before you were born. How do you know about it?" She looked at me as if I had asked a silly question. "My grandmother told me all about her," she said. There you have an example of the point I was making about the clear minds of elderly relatives!

4 • Family Stories

Family stories are the stuff of which dreams are made, the foundation of your search for your roots, and most unfortunately they are very often untrue. Let me make it clear that some family stories are quite accurate. As far as the other kind are concerned, I am not suggesting you come from a long line of congenital liars. It is simply that, human nature being what it is, a certain amount of decoration can creep in over the years. Stories are improved, vague and distant memories become "facts."

Be very cautious about any story which touches on the social standing of the family, because this is the biggest area of decoration. The farm laborer becomes a farmer, the sergeant in the army becomes a colonel, the cottage becomes a thirty-room mansion. Let's face it, this sort of thing happens today. Someone arrives in a new country, or a new city, makes new friends and tries to impress them a little with some slightly "improved" stories about his or her background.

"I'm so glad to have a smaller house. Our last one was really too much for me, even though I had a cleaning woman in for a couple of hours every day. I'm looking forward to having more time for myself. I was on so many committees it wasn't funny—PTA, opera, library board, volunteer work at the church. Everyone said I should have stood for election to the town council. I'm sure I would have been elected if this move of my husband's hadn't come along."

And so the stories grow! I know one family in England that has a lovely one. Great-grandfather had been the captain of a sailing vessel which crossed and re-crossed the stormy Atlantic from England to Boston, Massachusetts. The family were very proud of this brave old sea-dog of an ancestor, and, since several present-day members of the family liked "mucking about with boats," they were convinced this love of the sea had been handed down from great-grandfather. A couple of years ago a member of the family decided to trace his ancestors, and his search eventually took him back to this tough old ancestor, but he ran into an unexpected twist in the road. Great-grandfather had been a captain alright, but he had been a captain of a barge which went up and down the River Ouse, outside the port of Boston, in Lincolnshire, in England! Alas, for dreams of riding out the grim Atlantic storms! There was the slightest basis of truth, but all the rest was decoration—accidental, I'm sure— which had been added over the years.

Sometimes the decoration can be very deliberate. Many years ago I knew a couple of English immigrants in Canada. The husband had told me how he and his wife had grown up in the same poor neighborhood in the East End of London, and how they had gradually prospered to a limited degree, and had then decided to emigrate. A couple of years later I happened to be within earshot of the wife at a cocktail party and was amused to hear her saying, "Of course, I was brought up in the country in England. My parents were independently wealthy and we had a large house in Oxfordshire. It was an Elizabethan manor house, actually. We entertained a great deal and the local Hunt always started the season with a Meet at our house, when it was always my job to give the Master his stirrup-cup." It was a delightful story and I am sure her listeners believed her, but, of course, it was a pack of lies.

Stories of noble descent should always be very suspect. Ninety-five percent of your ancestors and mine were connected with the land: they were farmers (some, yeomen owning their own land, and some, tenant farmers renting their farm from the local big landowner), or they were blacksmiths, or farriers, or thatchers, or plowmen, or shepherds, or stablemen, or shearers, or any of the other jobs connected with agriculture and the countryside. They did not have titles or great wealth; they were honest working men and women. If you are descended from a titled family, the probability is that you will already have documentary proof within your family. If you don't, then work steadily back in the normal way and perhaps you will discover an aristocrat in your ancestry—if this is important to you!

These stories usually start accidentally and improve with the passage of time. Someone may have said to your grandmother: "Your maiden name was Howard? Are you any relation of the Duke of Norfolk?" And grandmother may have replied, "Who knows? Maybe I am!" Your Aunt Elizabeth, as a small child, may have overheard the conversation, liked the thought, and it became, "Mother said we were related to the Duke of Norfolk."

When you are discussing a place of birth or origin be very sure you get the name right. Double check with one more person at least, and don't assume the name you have been given is the name of a city or a village. It may be the name of a farm or a district or a county. Remember, too, that people, when asked for their place of birth in casual conversation, often give the name of the nearest big city rather than that of their small and unknown village.

As an example, a man named Wilhelm Müller was actually born in a village named Erlangen, on the outskirts of Nürnberg, but it was so much a part of the city that he always told the family he came from Nürnberg. So if you accepted this story without any attempt to prove it, you would be searching for your Müller ancestors in the wrong place.

On the other hand, let us suppose that Wilhelm Müller *was* born in Nürnberg, but as an old man he was a little vague about his date of birth. He always said it was 1880, and so his son put that date on his tombstone. In fact, he was born in 1878. Here again you would create a dead-end because you confused belief with fact.

If you are lucky enough to have the elderly aunt I mentioned earlier, or any other relative or family friend who is very old, handle him or her with tender, loving care. Don't suddenly arrive out of the blue—all hot and eager—complete with tape-recorder and a barrage of questions fired off as rapidly as an MK machine-gun. Older people don't like tape-recorders, nor does the human mind react favorably to cross-examination. Take your small notebook, sit and chat quietly, and start off by talking in generalities. Compliment Great-Aunt Jane on her youthful appearance, tell her you hope you'll look as good when you reach her great age, and then introduce the question of family history very gently. Once started, let her take the lead in the conversation—occasionally prompted by a short question if there is a suitable pause. DON'T INTERRUPT. What seems to you to be a wandering monologue may be a valuable and detailed narrative following a pattern all its own!

Take notes quietly, be prepared to let your informant wander a little, and don't overtire her by staying too long. Say, "Thank you," tell her how wonderful her help has been, tell her you would like to talk to her again in a couple of weeks, and ask her to jot down any other information she remembers in the interval. BE SURE YOU GO BACK because I guarantee you will get more information on the second visit. If you have been kind and charming, and have made a good impression, she will have been flattered by your interest and pleased that someone has listened to her. You have probably been the first person she has talked to about her family and herself for quite a long time.

When you get home, and while the conversation is fresh in your mind, go over your notes, expand them, add to them, and make sure you write down who gave you all the information, and when. Do this with all your conversations with relatives and family friends, because you may want to check back with them to clear up a question, and it will be infuriating if you don't know who gave you the details in the first place.

While we are talking about family members and the information they can give you, let me remind you of some remarks I made earlier about resistance to your questions. This can be a major obstacle, but often information which is withheld by one member can be obtained from another.

From my own experience of talking to hundreds of people at my meetings, or on TV and radio shows, the main cause of reluctance to talk about family is this irrational fear of an illegitimate ancestor. Maybe grandfather or great-grandfather was a bastard, or "born out of wedlock," or, to say it nicely, "he was a love child," but the odds are he was nothing of the kind.

In searching church registers you rarely find any evidence of bastard births. This is because our ancestors were brought up in a deeply religious society with a strict code of conduct, and social pressures were so strong that the "guilty" couple were hastily married when the pregnancy became evident. If a rushed marriage was not possible because the father of the child was already married, the entry of baptism of the child in the register usually reads: "Baptized this day, James, son of Mary Williamson, spinster. Admitted father, Thomas Nelson." There were no secrets in a small village. If you find an entry like this, the solution is simple. In your family tree put the marriage mark = between Mary Williamson and Thomas Nelson and start tracing the Nelsons back. Who is to know, except you, that the union was a little flawed and, after all, you have the Nelson blood in your veins. The fact that Thomas had a roving eye doesn't make him any less an ancestor!

I am always fascinated by the fact that clergymen were Christian enough to baptize every illegitimate child but quite often made a personal comment beside the entry in the register. I remember an entry I found in a Presbyterian church register in a parish in Scotland: "Baptised this day, Alexander, bastard son of Alison Spence and James Todd, conceived in utter filth and carnal lust." Nice man!

So what will you be asking your family and friends? You will want to know dates and places of birth or baptism, marriage, and death or burial. You will need to know your family religion, AND—most important—if this has changed within memory because of marriage, conversion, or some other cause. You should try and discover the occupation of your immediate for-bears—in this country and overseas, if he or she is a recent immigrant. You will want to know the country of origin and, if possible, the exact place and the approximate date of arrival over here if emigration took place.

Sometimes—but not often—someone from Scotland might give their country of origin as NB, meaning North Britain. If they came from one of the many ethnic areas once contained within the old Austro-Hungarian Empire, such as Slovakia, Bohemia, Croatia, or Slovenia, they might have simply written "Austria."

Depending on the individual circumstances of your family you should also discover what you can about name changes, naturalization, military service, apprenticeship to a craft, and ethnic background. All this information will help when you start looking through the records we will be talking about very soon.

When you have met or corresponded with all members of your immediate family, or old family friends, you must be sure to widen your area of research to include cousins. I repeat what I mentioned earlier: one member of your family may have vital information not known by anyone else, so if you know you have distant relatives in California or Canada, Austria or Australia, Florida or Finland, run them to earth and find out what they know. When you write—if they are strangers to you —make sure you explain you are tracing your ancestors, and that is your only aim. Otherwise—and this is a true story—you may get a letter back which says, "Why are you asking me all these questions? Have you discovered some missing money? If you have, I want my share!" There is greed and avarice just below the surface in many people!

Finally, you must be sure you do not make the greatest mis-take of all, which is to fail to check if someone has already traced your ancestors. You can do this in a number of different ways and we will come to them later.

Two items within your family will be very important to you if they exist—the family Bible and the family album. Up until about 1900 it was the custom to give a Bible to a newly married couple. There was space for entries of all the vital events to be recorded as they occurred—baptisms, marriages, burials. The Bible entries can be invaluable to you IF they were recorded as they occurred. On the other hand, if you find the entries are all recorded in exactly the same handwriting, with no variation for increasing age, then they were made later from hearsay and are suspect. The family album contains lots of photographs of stern looking men and women who are certainly your ancestors, but no one has written their names below. An elderly relative may be able to identify them for you, but if not, the only value is in the name and city of the photographer, so look at the back of the photographs. If you do find this information, it may well be the place of origin of your ancestor. He or she may have brought the picture to this country, or it may have been sent to them by the family after they emigrated. I know a number of cases where people have solved the puzzle of their family's place of origin by the information on the back of a faded photograph.

5 • Names

This is an area of research which can often lead you astray —both first names and surnames. I have heard people say quite seriously that all people with the same name would find they were related if they went back far enough. This is absolute nonsense. Surnames have a variety of origins, but in the main they are based on occupation, location, appearance, a mother, a father, and, sometimes, on an event occurring at the time of birth.

Surnames rarely existed before about 1300 in western countries. People simply had a first name followed by an identification to distinguish them from others. In a village you could find John the baker, John the fletcher, John the butcher, John the cooper, John of the hill, John by the wood, John in the dale, John of the flood, John of the storm—the list is almost endless. Eventually, with the increase of population, the system became clumsy and complicated, and the "ofs" and "thes" were dropped and surnames came into being as we know them today—except that there were tremendous variations in spelling. In the days before formal education, spelling depended on phonetics, or how a word sounded to the ear. In the same way that some people are tone-deaf to music, so others are tone-deaf to speech and pronunciation, so a simple name like Pearce could be spelt Perce, Peirs, Peirce, Peirse, or Pearse. Pearce itself originated with someone who was a son of a man named Piers (or Peter) and was known as Piers' son. This became shortened to Pearson or Pearce.

The origin of names, therefore, shows that all people with the same name are not necessarily related however far back you go. Take my name of Baxter, for example. It was originally an Old English, or Saxon, word meaning a baker, and was spelt Baecestre. From this there developed a variety of spelling over the centuries, and in my family tree can be found Backster, Bakster, Bacaster, Bacastar, Bacstar, Bagster, Bacchuster, Baster, and Bastar (this one I didn't like so much!).

In the Scandinavian countries, and parts of the Netherlands, and a small area in the north of what is now called Germany, a different system was common—patronymics and matronymics. The surname borne by the child was based on the first name of the father or mother, so Lars, the son of Jen would be known as Lars Jensen. Fortunately, in most cases, the minister officiating at a vital event—baptism, marriage, burial—would usually include the father or mother's surname with the words (in the appropriate language) "also known as." In Norway, in particular, there is an added complication. If a man bought a farm he would change his surname to the name of the farm; if he inherited a farm the same rule would apply. Matters could be still more complicated by the fact that if he took his head plowman or another worker with him, that man might also change his name to that of the farm! Ancestor-hunting does have its problems in Scandinavia, but as you will find out as you trace back, they can usually be overcome.

A few surnames, taken at random, are listed opposite to give you an idea of the origins on which they are based:

ENGLAND

Ackerman: Plowman

Bacon: Nickname for a butcher

Cantle: Dweller on point of land

Denham: Dweller at farm in valley

Emson: Son of Emma

Farnfield: Dweller by the ferns

Gill: Dweller in the ravine

Halliwell: Dweller by the holy well

Inwood: Dweller in a nearby wood

Jarvis: Man from Jervaulx (York)

Kershaw: Dweller in church wood

Leadbitter: A worker in lead

Marshall: A horse herder, or tender

Norton: Man from north of village

Osler: A bird catcher

Pannell: A saddle-maker

Quantrell: A dandy

Ringer: A presser of cheese

Shaw: Dweller by the wood

Tozer: A comber of wool

Uprichard: Son of Richard

Venner: Huntsman

Waite: A watchman

Yates: A gate-keeper

Zouch: Dweller by tree stump

EUROPE

Abreu (Portugal): Born in spring

Belli (Italy): Good looking

Charbonneau (France): Coal seller

Dabrowski (Poland): Dweller in oak wood

Eklund (Sweden): ditto

Felber (Germany): Dweller by willow tree

Gagnier (France): Farm owner

Haller (Germany): Man from city of Halle

Ivarsaon (Norway): Son of Ivar

Joder (Germany): Gift of God

Kenner (Germany): Man from canal bank

Lanza (Italy): Lancer in the army

Madsen (Denmark): Son of the strong man

Neri (Italy): Born in summer

Oliva (Spain): Dweller by olive tree

Pellegrini (Italy): Pilgrim

Quintero (Spain): A farmer

Ramos (Spain): Man of the forest

Szabo (Hungary): Tailor

Ten Eyck (Netherlands): At the oak tree

Ulman (Germany): Rich man

Vest (Norway): Man from the wood

Weber (Germany): A weaver

Yeager (Germany): Game hunter

Ziegler (Germany): Tile maker

First, or Christian, names naturally do not present as many problems as surnames, but they can still present difficulties and there are several things to watch for:

(1) If you are told that your grandfather's name is John Hammond, try and make sure that John was his *first* name and not his second. It is by no means unusual for someone to dislike his first name so much that quite early in life he drops all use of it and changes to the use of his second. As a matter of fact, I am a good example of this sort of thing. I happen to have a Christian name *before* the name Angus. I loathed and detested the name from a very early age, and when I was fourteen I announced to my mother that in future I would be known by my second name, Angus, and the loathsome first name would be buried forever. Should there be any descendants of mine a century ahead who start to try and trace back to me, I think they may have quite a problem! But, as Archie Bunker said, "What has posterity ever done for me?"

(2) Make very sure that the name of your grandfather or grandmother is not a diminutive, or pet, name. If grandmother's name in the family was Jenny, remember her baptismal name could have been Jane or Janet. There are other examples— Fanny could be Frances, Sally could be Sarah, Betsy could be Elizabeth, Nelly could be Helen, Frank could be Francis, Fred could be Alfred. The same problem arises in Europe, particularly in the Germanic area, where Seppi could be Joszef, Hansi could be Johann, Henni could be Heinrich, Lise could be Elisabeth. You will find many other examples of diminutives besides these.

If you are of European descent you should check very carefully into the accuracy of both first names and surnames. Quite often your immigrant ancestors anglicized or simplified these names; sometimes the change was made for them by some bigot of an immigration officer on Ellis Island or at some other port of entry in Canada or the United States. I know one true story about this sort of thing.

Back in the last century a Polish immigrant on the Island reached the table of an immigration officer and the following dialogue took place:

"Name?"

"Stefan Pryzyborski."

"What name?"

"Stefan Pryzyborski."

"What sort of name is that for America!

I'll call you Stanley Price. Next!"

So the USA had a new immigrant, and the immigrant had a new name—two new names in fact. So check naturalization papers or any other document in your family which can help to prove the accuracy of your surname. If you do have any personal papers that belonged to your immigrant ancestor, two very useful things to look for will be his military identity papers and his discharge book. In almost all European countries all males had to serve in the army for periods of one year or two —it varied from country to country. Emigrants were not allowed to leave the country unless they could produce evidence that they had completed their military service.

6 • Places

If you have read this far, you will have realized that the next most important fact you have to establish after names is the place from which your family originated. Sometimes this is no problem—the evidence is within the family, on paper, or in someone's memory. Sometimes it is extremely hard to find the information. Sometimes you will not be able to find the name of the place. This is rare, but it can happen.

Someone in the family may come up with an immediate answer, but before you get too excited, act as if your ancestors came from Missouri. Be cautious, and check very thoroughly. The name of the place you have been given may not be the name of a town or a village; it may be a county, or kreise, or bezirke, or oblastny—depending on the country. If your ancestors are Irish the place name may be a townland or a barony. It may even be the name of a farm.

Forty years ago when I started blundering about in search of my roots, and doing all sorts of stupid things in the process, I was led completely astray about the place of origin of my family. I told you earlier how cold the trail was when I started —father dead, grandparents dead, no books to guide me. I remember the first thing I did was to find a couple of famous people named Baxter and try and trace them down to me! I told you I was stupid. Then I looked up a book about surnames, and Baxter was described as a Scots surname. This was true enough, but the book should also have said it was an English name as well.

However, I accepted the information as true and so became quite certain I was of Scots descent, based on what the book had said. I was not led astray by my Christian name of Angus as I knew I had been named after a family friend. Then I found, with a lot of detective work, an old lady who was some kind of connection by marriage. When I asked her where the Baxter family came from, she said, "I think when I was a child I heard someone say they came from Tabert, or some such place." I had never heard of Tabert, but in Scotland there was a place in Argyll named Ta*r*bert, and, after all, I was Scots, wasn't I? The book said so. I said to her, "Could it have been Tarbert, in Scotland?" She replied, "Well, it could have been, couldn't it?"

This was enough for me and off I dashed to Scotland, to Tarbert, in the county of Argyll. I sat down with great eagerness and the certainty that I would find my ancestors recorded in the church registers. I painstakingly checked back for 200 years and no Baxters were mentioned. While I was in the area I looked through the registers of a couple of nearby parishes and got the same result. It was at this point I took a good hard look at myself and decided I must go back to square one and start with me, and believe only what I could document, and not what I was told. Incidentally, some long time later I found that in the late 1700s one of the farms my ancestors owned was named Ta*l*bert, so the story had a slight basis in fact, and I had further complicated matters by accepting the story as gospel— by believing what I read about the name—and by rushing off without any real evidence to justify my journey.

There are other problems in connection with the right identification of places, but they can all be overcome:

(1) You may find that although you have documentary proof that a particular place-name you have for your family's origin is correct, you cannot find any mention of the place on

maps or in gazetteers. The explanation is probably that the place has been absorbed into the nearest big city and has lost its own identity. You can always check this by writing to the archives of the country concerned.

(2) If you are of European descent, the above remarks apply, but you have an additional complication. Boundaries of countries have changed frequently because of various wars, and this means that the name of the village or town will have changed its name. If your family came from Allenstein, in Germany, you will now be dealing with Olsztyn, in Poland; Leitmeritz is now Litomerice in Czechoslovakia; Bozen, in Austria, is now Bolzano in Italy; Temisvár, in Hungary, is now Timisoara in Romania; Munkács, in Hungary, is now Muka-chëvo in the USSR. The list is a very lengthy one and I list these places as just a very few examples. Place-names can also change within a country for political reasons: Chemnitz, now in East Germany, has been re-named Karl-Marx-Stadt; Stalingrad, in the USSR, is now Volgograd.

(3) You may know for sure that great-grandfather was born in a particular parish, but you cannot find the parish or you cannot find grandfather. This may well be because the parish boundaries have been changed. Quite often a parish would be split in two because of a great increase of population in the area. In such a case the original name may be retained by one half and a new name given to the other half. Alternatively, both the new parishes may have been given new names and the old name will have disappeared.

Your search may also be affected by changes in county boundaries. In England, for example, the county of Yorkshire has been divided into five new counties—Cleveland, Humber-side, North Yorkshire, South Yorkshire, and West Yorkshire. In Denmark, the island of Fyn had two counties—Odense and Svendborg—now it has one named Fyn. The island of Moen had five counties—now reduced to two (Kobenhavns and Frederiksborg).

The archives of a country can supply you with information if you run into problems like this, and they will only be problems for a very short time.

An extreme example of what can happen because of boundary changes can be seen with Silesia. Teschen (Tesin in Czech, Cieszyn in Polish) is a former principality and town in that area of Europe. It has had a checkered history. It was under Bohemia from 1292 to 1625, then under Austria until 1918. In 1920 the western part was given to Czechoslovakia and the eastern part to Poland. The town of Teschen was also divided; the eastern part became Cieszyn and the western part Cesky Tesin in Czechoslovakia. Poland seized the latter section in 1938, Germany occupied both sections from 1939 to 1945, and then the boundaries reverted to those of 1920.

All this, genealogically, means that a Wilhelm Müller, born in Herrengasse, Teschen, in 1912 and living in the same house all his life, was Austrian at birth and Czechoslovak at his marriage in 1936, and that his children, born in 1937, 1939, and 1940, were respectively Czechoslovak, Polish, and German.

7 • The LDS Church

This seems to be the right place to talk about the LDS Church and its vast genealogical collection. Without any question at all, you will be dealing with these records at the very start of your search. The Church of Jesus Christ of Latter-day Saints—the LDS Church for short—is also known as the Mormon Church, but the members prefer the shorter name. Its records are available for use by those of us who are not members of the Church and there are no strings attached. Just because you use its resources does not mean anyone will try and convert you—no Church elder will arrive on your door-step. This will not happen.

I mentioned earlier in this book the importance of making sure no one has already researched your family. You can do this by asking for information from the local library in the place from which your family emigrated, or in the place in this country where the family settled. You should also contact the genealogical organizations in these two areas.

Above all, though, you should check the LDS Church records—either by writing directly to the Family History Library, 35 North West Temple Street, Salt Like City, Utah 84150, or by visiting or writing the nearest LDS branch library to where you live. There will be one not far away and you can always find the address through your nearest public library.

The interest of Church members in genealogy comes from their belief that family relationships are eternal, and not limited to the short period of time we spend on this earth. It is believed that husband and wife and their children remain together through eternity as a family unit, with their ancestors and descendants. Members of the Church trace their ancestors in order to perform "sealing" ceremonies in temples erected for this purpose. Before the families can be "sealed" together, all the ancestors must be traced.

The Genealogical Society of the LDS Church is engaged in the most active and comprehensive genealogical research program ever known. Microfilming and computerization are the heart of the operation, and every day records are being copied in some thirty-eight different countries around the world. There are more than a million rolls of microfilm in the Family History Library in Salt Lake City, covering such records as church registers, civil registration, census returns, land grants, deeds, military records, and cemetery and tombstone inscriptions. Thirty thousand new rolls are added each year. Over 200,000 printed volumes line the shelves, and more than 300 new books join them each month. There are records of ten million families in the archives, and more than sixty million names in the International Genealogical Index. These figures are staggering, and are very probably out-of-date already because the rate of increase is phenomenal.

The records vault—with copies of every item of genealogical information which the Church possesses—is located in the Rockies under 300 feet of solid granite. The total vault capacity—the equivalent of over twenty-six million volumes of 300 pages each—can be expanded through further excavation.

If you cannot visit the library in Salt Lake City—3,000 people do every day—you have access to all the records through your nearest LDS branch library. The main sources of information available to you are:

(1) The Family Group Records Collection. This consists of ten million family record forms from all over the world.

There is also the Family Registry. People doing family research have submitted the names of those they are tracing, and they are listed on microfiche in each branch library. If you look up your ancestor's name you can contact the person who submitted it (if it is there).

(2) The Family History Library Catalog. The catalog to the books in the library is on microfiche in your nearest branch library, and by checking this you can find out if the history of your family has already been published or is available in manuscript form.

(3) The International Genealogical Index (IGI). This is a computerized index to names extracted from various records. The main source of information in the IGI is the church register. This records baptisms, marriages, and burials, but so far as the LDS Church is concerned the emphasis is on baptisms and marriages. The registers of many different religions in many different countries have been copied, and the work is still proceeding. Bear in mind that not *all* registers have been copied, and not *all* religious organizations are prepared to co-operate with the LDS Church in this project.

Lack of knowledge about this can lead to a lot of confusion. I have heard from many people at various times: "I don't understand it. I know my ancestors came from such-and-such a place in such-and-such a county, and yet they are not listed in the IGI." The answer is simple—the Index is only based on the church registers copied. In England, for example, LDS workers have copied 100% of the registers of the county of Wiltshire, but only 3% of those in the county of Somerset. At this moment the registers for Cheshire, Kent, Middlesex, and Northampton have not been filmed at all because permission has not been given by the Church of England bishops with jurisdiction in these particular areas. Some of the registers in these four counties have already been published by the Parish Register Society or other organizations, and these, of course, the LDS Church has been able to copy, but they are only a tiny percentage of the whole.

When using the LDS records always remember that the copies are not 100% accurate. It has been known for mistakes to be made in names, or for several pages of a church register to be missed. The LDS records are vast, they are superb, but they are not the final word, nor will they ever be. Use them as a guide, but always be prepared to check the original records yourself.

There has been extensive microfilming of records from some European countries, notably Austria, Belgium, Denmark, Finland, France, Germany, Hungary, Iceland, the Netherlands, Norway, Poland, Sweden, and Switzerland. There is also some work being done in Portugal and Czechoslovakia. Generally speaking, the European coverage is not as comprehensive as that of North America and the United Kingdom and Ireland.

The LDS Church will not undertake research for you. If, for any reason, you are unable to visit a branch library to do it yourself, they will give you a list of professional researchers who are experts in your area of interest, and you can then make your own arrangements.

I should, perhaps, give you an example of a mistake I came across in the IGI. It was not important to me because I already had the particular information from the original church register, but if I hadn't, my research would have come to a sudden end.

A good many years ago I was tracing back my Caley ancestors in the northern part of the county of Lancashire, in England. I was living over there at that time and so was able to settle down in the area for a few days and do my searching in the various church registers. (This was in the days before the registers were transferred to the County Record Offices, and before many registers had been copied by the LDS Church.) I eventually traced back to a Henry Caley (died 1819) who married an Ellen Webster in 1778 in a village named Cockerham. I could not get back any further because Henry had not been born in the village—he had arrived there out of the blue and bought a farm and a couple of years later married a local girl. I searched all the registers of the adjoining parishes and the name Caley did not appear anywhere.

Over the years I have made sporadic searches of other records—land records, taxes, deeds, manorial rolls, etc.— without any success. A few years ago I noticed that the LDS Church had copied 48% of the parish registers of the county, including the parish of Cockerham. I got a print-out of the Caley entries for the county (it cost me 50¢ a sheet for about twenty sheets), but there was no entry of birth of a Henry Caley which could by any possibility be my Henry Caley, and so that was another dead-end.

However, quite casually I looked through the marriage entries and found that the marriage of Henry Caley and Ellen Webster on 25 November 1778 was not listed! I knew this was wrong because I had seen the entry in the church register with my own eyes. I looked further down the list and found another entry which showed the marriage of a *Thomas* Caley to Ellen Webster on that same date and in that same place! I thought, "Could I possibly have made a mistake?" And so I wrote off to the County Record Office in Lancashire (which now held the register) and asked the archivist to check the register for me, explaining the reason. He replied and told me I was correct and the LDS Church was wrong. I notified Salt Lake City and, in due course, they replied, admitted the error, apologized, and said the correction would be made in the next issue of the IGI for Lancashire. Sure enough, two years later, Henry's marriage to Ellen Webster appeared. There was only one problem—they had left in the fictitious Thomas's marriage. I wrote again and pointed this out, and I was assured the deletion would be made in the next issue. In fact, it was not. I did not bother any more and, so far as I know, mythical Thomas is still gracing the IGI for Lancashire!

This error was not of major importance for me because I had already done my searching before I bought the print-out, but if I had not I would have been led away from the beaten track. This is not a criticism of LDS records—in general they are a tremendous help to all of us tracing our ancestors—but mistakes are obviously made, so do not accept the church records in Salt Lake City as absolutely accurate. Be sure you check original sources as well.

Important Note
Before You Read Chapters 8 to 12

In the next five chapters we will be talking about various sources of information—the major ones of civil registration, census returns, church registers, and wills—and some minor ones which may well turn out to be of major value to you. However, I will only be covering a few countries in a very abbreviated form. You will need to read one or other of my four published books to get all the information in detail.

To obtain information about your ancestors from these various sources you will almost certainly be involved in writing letters to various organizations and individuals in this country and abroad. Whether you get an answer or not may well depend on four actions you must take. These actions are of vital importance in getting off to a good start in your ancestral search:

(1) When you write for information to any source, write a nice, friendly letter, and don't be abrupt and demanding. Please remember that no one *has* to answer your letter, and if you are unpleasant you will not get a reply. You will say at this point, "What a totally unnecessary piece of advice! I always write polite letters!" I am delighted to hear that you do, but you should see some of the extraordinary letters people in this country and abroad receive from ancestor-hunters. As you may imagine, with my books being published in four countries, I get a great many letters asking me for information or advice. I

also have my share of the rude ones —"My grandfather emigrated from the USA to Canada in 1855. Send me his family tree at once." "My grandmother came from Canada. Tell me what you know about her." "Make that priest at Huit-Iles answer me."

(2) If you are writing to anyone in the country of your family's origin in Europe, try and write in the language of the country. If you have lost your ancestral language, and cannot get a relative or friend to translate for you, then write in English. Good English is better than bad German or Polish or Italian or whatever! If you are writing in English, apologize in your letter for your inability to speak the language of the country. Generally speaking there is no great problem in writing in English to the Scandinavian countries, the Netherlands, Belgium, Germany (the FDR), or Switzerland.

(3) ALWAYS cover the return postage, whether you are writing to government departments, local municipalities, archives, libraries, genealogical or family history societies, clergymen, burial grounds, or any other source of information. Remember, you are not the only ancestor-hunter writing a letter—there are tens of thousands of you! I know one County Record Office in England which, in 1986, received over 10,000 letters from overseas, and only 500 included return postage! That is why the general rule has become, "No return postage, no reply." So—remember to do this and also to send a self-addressed airmail envelope. You can cover the return postage in one of two ways so far as overseas correspondence is concerned:

(a) You can go into your local post office and buy *two* International Reply Coupons and send them with your letter. The recipient can then exchange these at a post office "over there" for sufficient stamps for an airmail reply to you. I will not quote costs of coupons to you because the price will probably have increased by the time you read this. You will certainly pay twice as much as you would expect!

(b) However, if you know you are about to start sending a number of letters of enquiry to "the old country," you can save half your costs by writing to the Central Post Office of any major city in the country to which you are going to write, and say: "I enclose in cash fifty marks or fifty francs or ten pounds (or whatever the currency is). Please send me the equivalent value in the right denomination for stamps for airmail postage from your country to mine." This will be about 50% cheaper than buying two IRCs every time you write. Note I say *in cash*. If you send a bank draft or dollars the bank over there will charge a large fee for exchange, and the whole idea will not be worth bothering about. If you do not care to risk sending cash then follow the procedure in (a) above and use IRCs. I have never lost cash in the mail, but I suppose there is always a first time! Any bank or currency dealer will obtain cash for you.

So far as correspondence within this country is concerned, of course, you simply stick a stamp of the right value on the self-addressed envelope you are enclosing. If you expect any enclosure such as a certificate or a photo-copy to be sent back to you, then be sure the envelope you enclose for the reply is a business-size one (known as a no. 9 or no. 10).

(4) When you are writing for information be brief, be clear; type your letter or write very clearly; quote accurate names and dates and places (if you know them). List the sources you have checked already. DO NOT write a long "letter from home"— your own family is absolutely fascinating to you, but the person who reads your letter has heard it all many times before and will become very impatient if he or she has to wade through pages of family stories.

If you will remember these four pieces of advice then you are certain to get replies and fairly certain to obtain some information of value to you.

8 • Civil Registration

This is the compulsory registration of births, marriages, and deaths. Before the introduction of this type of record-keeping, all information about these "vital events" is to be found in church registers of various denominations. The date of the start of civil registration varies greatly from country to country, and even within the states and provinces and districts of each country.

I will be telling you about starting dates in a limited number of countries, but you must appreciate that this does not mean that everyone was law-abiding and started to register the family events from the very first day they were supposed to do so. It took several years before civil registration was as automatic as it is today. There were a variety of reasons for this. In many countries there was deep suspicion about the motives of the government in introducing such a revolutionary idea. It was an invasion of personal privacy. The information could be used to find tax-evaders. The registration of deaths could be used as a basis for the collection of death duties. The registration of births could be used as a basis for later conscription of males for military service. Some of these suspicions were well-founded.

Apart from all these reasons there were other more down-to-earth ones. A century or a century-and-a-half ago people lived under different conditions than today. Many of them lived in isolated areas, and travel to the nearest village or town to register an event would have been almost impossible because of lack of public transport; people could not all read or write and would be totally unaware of the new regulations; if a doctor was present at a birth he would register the event, but many births took place with only a midwife or a local woman or a relative on hand; a marriage could be performed by a clergyman who did not bother to register it; a death could be followed by a burial on a farm and go unrecorded.

United States: The starting date varies from state to state and you will have to check for yourself by writing to the state capital. One short-cut, however, is to consult Thomas J. Kemp's *Vital Records Handbook* (Baltimore: Genealogical Publishing Company, 1988) which provides addresses of vital records offices, starting dates of the records, fees, and application forms.

Canada: In this country there is variation from province to province. In Ontario civil registration started officially in 1869, in Alberta in 1897 (with many gaps before 1905), but in Québec there has been a form of civil registration through the local Catholic churches since 1621 and in Protestant churches since 1760. (Civil registration as we understand it today did not commence until 1926.)

England and Wales: The starting date for these two countries was 1 July 1837, and the indexes are complete to within the last twelve months. They cover the whole of the area in one alphabetical order for each quarterly volume. The LDS Church has now microfilmed these indexes for the period 1837-1903. This will make searching for information much easier, but you will still have to order a certificate of the entry from the General Register Office, St. Catherine's House, 10 Kingsway, London WC2B 6JP, or from the District Registry Office for the area in which you are interested. The fees charged for certificates seem to increase steadily and I cannot quote an accurate figure, but it will probably be about $20.

Scotland: Registration started in 1855. The LDS Church has copies of the indexes from 1855 to 1955 and copies of the actual certificates from 1855 to 1875. They are all on microfilm. The originals are in the General Register Office, New Register House, Edinburgh EH1 3YT. From a genealogical point of view the 1855 registration forms are magnificent. Unfortunately, the mass of information demanded and received took so much effort to record that in later years fewer questions were asked. The wealth of facts required is too long to list but if you have an ancestor born in Scotland in 1855, or a brother or sister, then the certificate will not only tell you about the child, but will list dates and places of birth of the parents, date and place of their marriage, and details of any brothers or sisters of the child.

Ireland: Although the country is now partitioned between Eire and Northern Ireland (six of the nine counties of Ulster), this partition took place years after civil registration commenced. The starting date was 1 January 1864, but records of Protestant marriages started on 1 April 1845. The records are in the office of the Registrar-General, The Custom House, Dublin, or in the Public Record Office of Northern Ireland (PRONI), in Belfast, which also has indexes of birth registers from 1864 to 1922 for the whole of Ireland.

France: Civil registration started in 1792. The records are located in the town or village of origin, with a copy in the Départementale Archives up to 1870 approximately, and since that date in the local court of the first instance (Greffe du Tribunal de Prèmiere Instance) located in the chief city of the Préfecture or Département. Both the town hall (mairie) and the archives have yearly and ten-year indexes, so there is no problem in tracing an entry if you have a name, date, and place to start with.

The system of genealogical record-keeping in France is unlike most other European countries. Once you understand it, you will find it very easy and reasonably inexpensive. The key to ancestor-hunting in France is the system used to maintain a permanent record of an individual during his or her life. For example, the civil registration records in the town hall have very wide margins. These are used for notes to be added later in order to update the information about the individual.

Since 1897 the birth certificate has shown in the margin the date and place of the subsequent marriage of the child, and since 1922 it has also shown the date and place of the marriage of the child's parents. Since 1945 the margin has also included details of the eventual death of the child. Be sure when you write that you ask for a "full certificate" (in French *copie littèrale*), otherwise you will receive an abridged version containing only the name or names and the date.

Germany: Civil registration started in 1875 following the unification of the country, but in many areas it had started earlier since the individual states had their own laws and systems of record-keeping. In those areas originally under French control, such as Alsace-Lorraine (Elsass-Lothringen) and a few other small areas west of the Rhine, it started in 1810; in Frankfurt 1850; in Lübeck and Oldenburg 1811; in Hanover (Hannover) 1809; and in most parts of Prussia (Preussen) 1870.

There is a Registry Office (Standesamt) for each particular area, and several of them in the larger cities. Outside the cities the registration areas can be quite large. There is no national index of names, and not even one on a state basis. A copy of the entry in the local offices is sent to the archives in each of the state capitals.

•   •   •

Even the official records in the different countries are not always reliable. A friend of mine had an amusing experience a few years ago in England. He knew the date of his grandfather's marriage but not his grandmother's surname. He also knew that his grandfather had been a sawyer—that is, a man who works with a saw in a lumber yard or saw mill. He sent off for a copy of the marriage certificate to St. Catherine's House, London, in order to find out his grandmother's maiden name. In due course, the copy of the marriage certificate arrived, but grandfather's occupation had changed from sawyer to lawyer. In this case the family's social standing was considerably improved by a slip of the pen or the typewriter. From such an occurrence there starts the story of legal eagles roosting in the family tree!

9 · Church Registers

Generally speaking the recording of vital events in churches started in the United Kingdom and in western Europe in the mid-1500s, although a few registers have been discovered that date back to the late 1300s. The amount of information recorded over the centuries depended very much on the whim of the clergymen. In some cases a baptismal entry includes the names of both parents and in other cases the name of the father only. In some instances the maiden name of the mother is also given. Remember that the date is that of the baptism or christening and not of the birth—although sometimes you will find that recorded as well. Marriages are usually well recorded with the names of both parties, but deaths are not recorded at all in certain periods—usually when the plague hit a parish and the clergyman was too busy conducting burial services to bother with records.

As far as North America is concerned the same remarks apply except that, of course, the starting date of the registers depended on the settlement of a particular area.

United States: There are very many denominations; many registers have been lost or destroyed; many churches have been closed, abandoned, or destroyed by fire or flood; custody of the registers varies from state to state and from church to church; and there is no common denominator. You will have to start with the local church or churches in the area in which you are interested and go on from there. You may find the original registers are still in the church, or they have been lodged with the state headquarters of the particular denomination, or in the state library or archives. In other cases, a local historical or genealogical society may have taken custody on behalf of the state. Be prepared to find that parish boundaries have changed several times over the years. If you experience problems on the local level you will find it is worthwhile going higher up the church hierarchy in the state or the nation. The LDS Church, of course, has microfilmed many of the registers.

Canada: The situation in Canada is very much the same as in the United States. No denomination has a *national* policy regarding the preservation of early registers. With the possible exception of the Catholic Church there is very little central control of individual places of worship. Occasional efforts are made to "persuade" individual clergymen to hand over their early registers to church archives for safekeeping, but even the persuasion varies in intensity from place to place. However, in the Toronto area the Catholic Church has allowed the LDS Church to microfilm all records of baptism and marriage from the earliest available date in each parish up to 1910. The burial records were also filmed in parishes where they existed. Other dioceses have refused any co-operation with the LDS Church, but are insisting on hand-written copies being prepared by each parish and lodged in the diocesan archives.

Naturally, the starting date of all registers of all the various denominations depends on the date of settlement and building of the first church or chapel. In the province of Québec this can be as early as 1620, whereas in Ontario there is very little before 1800.

You will find full information about the exact location of each early register (of all denominations) in my book *In Search of Your Roots,* available in Canada from Macmillan of Canada, 29 Birch Avenue, Toronto, Ontario M4V 1E2, and in the USA from the Genealogical Publishing Company, 1001 N. Calvert Street, Baltimore, Maryland 21202.

England and Wales: The starting date for Church of England parish registers is 5 September 1538. Some registers in a small village in Derbyshire named Crich date back to 1344, but this is quite exceptional. In 1538 all parsons were ordered to keep full records of baptisms, marriages, and burials. They were also ordered to keep the books in "a sure coffer with two locks." In 1598 all the entries were supposed to be copied into parchment books so that the paper books could be destroyed. The official act laid it down that the entries should be copied from the beginning, "but especially since the first year of Her Majesty's reign." In most cases this loose phrase was taken to mean that entries BEFORE the first year of the reign of Elizabeth I did not need to be copied, and so few records exist before 1558.

The act of 1598 also directed that each parson should—once every year—send a copy of all entries in the church registers to the diocesan registry (these are now known as Bishops' Transcripts). In many cases where registers have been lost or destroyed, these transcripts have been preserved. In my very early days of ancestor-hunting in a particular parish I was appalled to find that the registers were missing between 1634 and 1684. I was stuck for a year until, quite by chance, I found out about the Bishops' Transcripts—and these covered the missing fifty years. On occasion I have been astonished to find that even "expert" genealogists were unaware of them—so don't forget their existence. You will find them in the County Record Office, but more about this great source of information later.

If you are unlucky you may find both the registers and the transcripts are missing for the same period. This usually occurs between 1642 and 1660 when life was disrupted by the Civil War and the Cromwell regime. This is particularly true of the Midlands area of England, which was the scene of a great deal of the fighting between Cavaliers and Roundheads.

If your ancestors were members of the Church of England, the parish registers will provide you with vital information about them. By and large, there was not a great deal of movement of the population before the Industrial Revolution and the consequent drift to the mills and factories from the farms. This static population between 1558 and about 1790 meant that men and women were most likely to marry someone from their own village, or at least from the neighboring one or from the market town a few miles away. Their social life was based on the village green and the church, with, perhaps, an occasional visit to the nearest town for market day or the annual fair. If you are searching for the marriage of a particular ancestor and you fail to find him or her in the parish register, then turn your attention to the adjoining parishes and you are very likely to find the entry there.

If your ancestors were Catholic you may have more difficulty because at various times Catholics were forbidden to be baptized or married in their own church—the event had to take place in the parish church or it would not be legal. Some Catholics obeyed, but also had the baptism or marriage performed again in secret in their own church, or in a "safe" house, by a Catholic priest. Most of the records of the "secret" events are missing, but the Catholic registers are in the original churches, except in a few cases where they are in church archives. However, remember you will have to check Church of England registers as well as those of your own religion if your ancestors were Catholic.

The same remarks apply to all the Nonconformist religions and their many sects and schisms. Here, again, there were periods when they were compelled to have the vital events of the family recorded in the parish church. The Nonconformist registers are in the Public Record Office, in London, but most of the CROs (County Record Offices) have copies for their particular area.

Almost all the parish registers of England and Wales are now in the CROs and NOT in the original churches. In 1978 a new law directed that all parish registers be transferred there from the church—except in cases where the local church authorities could meet stringent regulations for temperature control, protection from weather, and security. As a result, only a very few registers have not been transferred.

Unfortunately, one of the causes of the law was the barbarity of a few ancestor-hunters who ripped out whole pages from registers when they found an ancestral entry. They should have been hanged from a branch of their family tree!

In the "good old days"— that is, about twenty-five years ago —a visit to a parish church to look through the registers was a very pleasant and civilized experience. You arrived on the doorstep of the parson's house, introduced yourself, and asked if you could look through the registers. You had to be prepared for difficult conditions such as standing up holding a heavy book in a drafty Norman tower; or sitting on a stool in an ill-lit vestry while the clergyman prowled up and down watching you. On the other hand, you could also be welcomed into the house, given a double Scotch, and settled down in a deep leather arm-chair in front of a roaring fire. All these things happened to me. One of the joys of such a visit was the opportunity to chat about the past and present life of the village with a keen observer of humanity and a lover of local history. Those days are gone beyond recall, and now you will sit at a table in a County Record Office and search the registers under the watchful eyes of the archival staff. One day soon you will not even see the registers—they will be on microfilm or microfiche. Oh, I know, the change is a good one; old registers will be preserved from damp and rot and theft and who can argue with the wisdom of it all?

I mentioned that a few registers are in the original churches. I hope you will not have to have any dealings with an infamous vicar of a church near London who charges the same fee for a certificate as St. Catherine's House, increases his rates when St. Catherine's House does, and allows no researcher anywhere near the registers!

Scotland: There is some evidence that registers were first kept in the fourteenth century, but none have survived so far as is known. In 1552 the General Provincial Council of Scotland ordered that each parish should maintain a register in which was recorded all baptisms and marriages, but this was only observed in a few parishes. In 1616 the newly formed Church of Scotland issued an edict that every minister should record baptisms, marriages, and burials. Again, few parishes took any action. In fact, only twenty-one parishes kept records before 1600, and thirty-five did not even start until 1801! Very few of the registers in Scotland have ever been printed or published, but everything is about to change. The LDS Church has copied the registers of every parish in Scotland from the earliest date up to 1855, when civil registration started. These are now being alphabetically indexed by name on a county basis. There are thirty-three counties and at the time of writing eighteen have been indexed. It is safe to say that by the time you read this the indexing for all the counties will have been completed, and, probably, an alphabetical index for the whole country as well.

The Microfilm Section of the General Register Office for Scotland, New Register House, Edinburgh EH1 3YT can supply a microfiche of the baptism and marriage entries for a particular surname in the counties copied by the LDS Church pre-1855. The cost is *about* $3 per fiche and the number you will require for a particular county depends on the number of people with that surname. If you tell them the county and the surname they will tell you the cost.

Remember that when we speak of the Church of Scotland we refer to the Presbyterian faith. The other religions in Scotland—both the Catholic Church and the Episcopal Church in Scotland (the religious equivalent of the Anglican Church)—have a policy of leaving their registers in the original churches.

Ireland: When you are searching church registers in Ireland you may well be dealing with both Eire and Northern Ireland, irrespective of where your ancestors originated.

By far the most popular religion in Eire is that of the Catholic Church. The two Protestant religions (the Church of Ireland and the Presbyterian Church) probably account for 12% of the population. In Northern Ireland the figures are probably 55% Protestant and 45% Catholic, although the statistics are disputed by one or the other.

There is great variation in the starting date of Catholic registers. Some go back as far as 1680 while many others are not available before 1850. From about 1700 to 1800 public worship by Catholics was prohibited, consequently many vital events were recorded in secret and the records were subsequently lost. The same remarks apply to Presbyterians. The Church of Ireland, however, has many registers which date back to the middle of the seventeenth century.

There is one major problem affecting any research you do with Church of Ireland registers. In 1870 the British Government in Dublin ordered all the early registers to be sent there for safekeeping in the Public Record Office. Over a thousand volumes were eventually sent and all but four were destroyed in a fire in the PRO in 1922. Fortunately, many clergymen had copies made before surrendering the originals, others obtained permission to retain the registers because they had secure facilities for doing so, and as a result some 600 Church of Ireland registers survive. These are of value to all denominations because many Catholics and Presbyterians were buried in the graveyard of the parish church. The majority of the Church of Ireland registers are in the Public Record Office in Dublin or in the Public Record Office in Belfast (for those churches located in Northern Ireland). However, there are also many registers still in the original churches in both sections of Ireland and no accurate list of them is available.

The Catholic registers are in the original churches in Eire, but copies on microfilm are in the National Library in Dublin. In Northern Ireland there are few registers left in the Catholic churches—most are in the Public Record Office in Belfast. Copies of almost all Presbyterian church registers for the

whole of Ireland are in the custody of the Presbyterian Historical Society, Fisherwick Place, Belfast. A useful tool for
determining the existence, location, and starting dates of the
registers of all denominations is Brian Mitchell's *A Guide to
Irish Parish Registers* (Baltimore: Genealogical Publishing
Company, 1988).

France: Baptismal records in the Catholic churches commenced in 1539, marriages in 1563, and deaths in 1579. The
registers up to 1792 are in the Archives Départementales, and
since that date in the original churches. You will need to know
the place from which your ancestors came and the Département
(county) in which it is located. There have been changes in
Département boundaries from time to time.

The Protestant registers are usually Lutheran from 1525 and
Calvinist from 1559. The locations of these records are widely
scattered—some in the local church, some in the mairies (town
halls), some in the Archives Départementales, some in the
Library of the Protestant Historical Society (54 rue des Saint-
Pères, Paris), and, for part of southern France, in the Archives
Départementales du Gard, 30040 Nimes).

Germany: Some church registers date back to the fifteenth
century, but you should not expect to find many of them before
1563, for Catholics, and a few years later for Lutherans. Some
of the exceptions are to be found in Baden and Württemberg
where there are Lutheran registers dating back to 1531 and
1545 respectively.

The registers are either in the original churches, the various
church archives, or the state archives. It is not possible to list all
the various locations, but you will find full details in my book
In Search of Your European Roots, published by the Genealogical Publishing Company, 1001 N. Calvert Street, Baltimore, Maryland 21202, and by Macmillan of Canada, 29
Birch Avenue, Toronto, Ontario M4V 1E2, Canada. There are
many other church records detailed in the book.

10 • Censuses

United States: These records are located in the National Archives in Washington, D.C., with copies in regional archives and very many public libraries (for their particular area). The first census was taken in 1790 and one has been taken every tenth year since then. The 1880 census is of great value since the state or country of origin of the parents had to be included. This, of course, is invaluable for anyone whose ancestors entered the country from 1790 onwards. The 1890 census was, in large part, lost by fire, and only fragments still exist. There are also gaps in the returns for 1790, 1800, and 1810. Census returns are available for public inspection up to 1910. Since that date they are closed to public search in order to respect the privacy of individuals still alive, but in certain circumstances information from later returns can be released on special application, with proof of relationship and an explanation of the reasons for the special request. The 1920 census will be open to public inspection in 1992.

When examining the census returns on microfilm you must be prepared for difficulties—the reproduction of writing which has faded with age, the bad handwriting of an enumerator, and the use of his own personal abbreviations. Early census returns only included the name of the head of the household—usually a man—plus a head count of the other occupants of the house. It was only in 1850 that every individual was described by sex, age, color, and name, with the birthplaces of the children.

I have mentioned the value of the 1880 census, but the 1900 census also includes a new and vital detail—the year of a person's immigration into the United States. With this most valuable information you can then turn to passenger lists and naturalization records.

You can, of course, borrow on microfilm through your local library (if it has a microfilm viewer) the census returns for anywhere in the United States. Copies are also available at any LDS branch library. The 1790 census has been completely indexed by the Bureau of the Census. Many local libraries and historical and genealogical societies have also indexed state and local censuses. For details of the censuses from 1790 to 1920, state-by-state and county-by-county, see William Thorndale and William Dollarhide's *Map Guide to the U.S. Federal Censuses, 1790-1920* (Baltimore: Genealogical Publishing Company, 1988).

Canada: Census taking in Canada started in 1851, covering Upper and Lower Canada (now the provinces of Ontario and Québec) and New Brunswick, and gradually extended across the country as new provinces were formed and older ones entered Confederation (Nova Scotia in 1871, and in 1881 Alberta, British Columbia, Manitoba, Saskatchewan, and Prince Edward Island). The former colony of Newfoundland, which joined Canada in 1949, had province-wide censuses in 1921, 1931, and 1945, and there were also various local ones as early as 1671. All Canadian census records available for public search are in the Public Archives of Canada, Ottawa, with copies in the various provincial archives and many local public libraries (1851-1891 inclusive).

England and Wales: Censuses commenced in 1841 and have been held every ten years since (except for 1941), and are available up to 1891. The information contained in the 1901 return can also be made available on special application and proof of descent. All returns are in the Public Record Office, Census Search Room, Land Registry Building, Portugal Street,

London WC2A 3HP. Most County Record Offices have copies for the county, and in many cases these have been indexed—in particular, the one for 1851 which contained a great deal of genealogical information.

Scotland: The information for England and Wales applies here as well, except that the records are in the General Register Office, New Register House, Edinburgh EH1 3YT. The census returns for the whole of Scotland for 1841-1891 have been copied by the LDS Church and are available through your nearest LDS branch library. They are not indexed, so you will need to know the location.

Ireland: A census of Protestants was taken in 1740, and another of both Protestants and Catholics in 1766. The originals have been destroyed but some copies exist in the Public Record Offices in Dublin and Belfast. Censuses were taken on a regular basis from 1821 but almost all of them for the period 1821-1851 were lost in the 1922 fire in the Four Courts Building in Dublin, and those for 1861-1891 were later destroyed by mistake. The returns for 1901 and 1911 are available in the PROs.

France: The first census was held as far back as 1590 in one area, and there were other censuses over the years in various places on a very haphazard basis so far as locality is concerned. Where the records exist they will either be in the Archives Départementales, or in the local mairie (town hall). Nationwide censuses have been held every five years since 1836 and the returns are in the archives mentioned above, with a copy in the mairie.

Germany: Censuses have been held since 1871 when the unified state of Germany came into existence. Copies of the returns are in the various municipal archives (Stadtarchiv) of each district or in the district registry office (Standesamt) so far as the Federal Republic of Germany (BRD) is concerned.

East Germany (DDR) destroys its census returns once they have been counted, but this policy seems likely to change. Earlier ones—before partition—are in the Stadtarchiv in each municipality.

You must be prepared to find that some returns were destroyed by bombing in World War II. It may be wise for you to contact the central census authority and ask if the census returns exist for a particular location in a particular year and where they are located. The addresses for the two sections of Germany are:

West Germany: Statistisches Bundesamt, Gustav Stresemann Ring 11, Postfach 5528, 6200 Wiesbaden, Bundesrepublik Deutschland.

East Germany: Statistik der DDR, Hans Beimlerstrasse 70-72, 1026 Berlin, Deutsche Demokratische Republik.

11 • Wills

Wills of your ancestors can be of tremendous value to you if they exist. Nowadays most of us make a will, but that was not the case a century ago. If your ancestor did not own property there was no point in making one. Even if he did, he may not have bothered. In a close-knit family the disposition of property and possessions was often decided within the family and, therefore, no will was made, and no fees were payable to a lawyer. Of course there were many people then—as there are today—who refuse to face the reality of their own inevitable death and put off the making of a will until it is too late. Their relatives are then left with all the legal problems of winding up the estate —at a considerable cost.

An ancestral will can often solve problems of relationship in areas of settlement where several brothers or cousins with the same surname were all producing children at the same time. It can also throw some light—however dim—on the character of your ancestor if he or she disinherited a child. Sometimes the will of an immigrant ancestor can give you a clue as to his place of origin in the old country. I know of one case where a will contained the bequest of a gold ring to a brother in Tromsoe, Norway. This was followed up by a present-day ancestor-hunter who had never known the place in Norway from which great-grandfather had emigrated. As a result he can now produce a family tree going back over two centuries because of one small item in a will.

United States: The location of wills varies from state to state but they can usually be found in county courthouses. You will have to pay a fee for the search and the photocopy. In the eastern states it is possible to find wills dating back to the seventeenth century. Wills are of value because often all members of a family are mentioned, and this may solve many problems. Detailed discussions of wills as a genealogical source are found in various publications, but perhaps the best treatment of the subject is in Val Greenwood's *Researcher's Guide to American Genealogy* (Baltimore: Genealogical Publishing Company, 1973) and Arlene Eakle and Johni Cerny's *The Source* (Salt Lake City: Ancestry Publishing Company, 1984).

Canada: There is so much variation in the location of wills from province to province that I can only suggest you read all the details in my book devoted to Canadian records *(In Search of Your Roots)*. If I listed here all the Canadian locations I would have to do the same thing for the United States, and that would be a tremendous task. Wills in Québec go back to the early seventeenth century, but in other provinces the date varies with that of settlement.

England and Wales: Wills became fairly common about 1550, but a surprising number are available as early as 1195. Until quite recently they were proved in ecclesiastical courts—which one depended in which diocese or see the deceased was living in at the time of death. Whole books have been written telling people how to discover the locations of wills. Not any more. Most wills up to 1858 are now lodged in their respective County Record Offices. Wills since that date are in the Principal Registry of the Family Division, Somerset House, Strand, London WC2R 1LP. There are some other locations as well—principally the Public Record Office, Chancery Lane, London WC2A 1LR, for the all-important probate records of the Prerogative Court of Canterbury—and these are set out in detail in my book *In Search of Your British and Irish Roots,* published in the USA by the Genealogical Publishing Company, Baltimore; in Canada by Macmillan of Canada, Toronto; and in Australia by Methuen Ltd., North Ryde, Sydney.

Scotland: Wills in Scotland date back to the fourteenth century and, as in England and Wales, they were originally the responsibility of the Church of Scotland. After the Reformation the church courts were abolished and replaced by courts in the various commissariot districts, as they were called. This system then continued until 1876 when the proving of wills passed to the sheriffs' courts. Many of the commissariot records have been indexed up to 1800 by the Scottish Record Society, and copies are in the various main libraries. All pre-1823 records are in the Scottish Record Office, General Register House, Edinburgh EH1 3YY.

The Scots legal system, particularly the various restrictions on the disposal of property, differs from England and Wales, and these differences are explained at some length in my book mentioned above.

Ireland: Virtually all the pre-1858 wills of Ireland were destroyed in the fire of 1922, but many wills had been indexed before that date, and so though the wills are gone beyond recall the indexes are available. There are also several collections of abstracts of wills and these are in the Genealogical Office, Dublin Castle, Dublin, and in the Public Record Office of Northern Ireland (PRONI) in Belfast. Most will books and indexes to wills after 1858 survived the fire, and these are now divided between the Public Record Office in Dublin and PRONI in Belfast.

France: Wills date from the fifteenth century and are in the Archives Nationales, Paris, and copies are in the Archives Départementales and also in the Archives Municipales in each city, town, and district.

Germany: The probate system in Germany is a little complicated. Once a will has been drawn up, a copy is deposited in
the district courthouse (Amtsgericht) for the area in which the
testator is *living*. The local authorities then notify the civil
registry office (Standesamt) in the district where the testator
was *born*. When he dies, the Standesamt in the place of death
notifies the Standesamt in the place of birth, and the latter, in
turn, notifies the court of law of the location of the will. The
court then executes the will and lodges it in the district courthouse and sends a copy to the state archives (Staatsarchiv) in
each state. In East Germany there is a variation. The will is
lodged in the office of the state notary in each county. For
earlier wills you should contact the Zentralstelle für Genealogie
in der Deutschen Demokratischen Republik, Georgi Dimitroff
Platz 1, 7010 Leipzig, DDR.

●   ●   ●

These are the most important sources of information in your
hunt for your ancestors, but there are others to follow in the
next chapter. Before we leave this one, however, there is one
more point to make about wills. When you have found the location of the will you will be able to get a photocopy for a few
cents. If your ancestor was able to write (and 200 or more
years ago few could) you will see his signature and can compare
it with your own, and see if there is any similarity. Much more
interesting is the fact that in those days possessions were
usually described in great detail—totally unlike present-day
wills. Here is an extract from the will of an ancestor of my
wife's, dated 1695:

> "In the name of God, Amen, the sixteenth day of
> February, in the year of our Lord God, 1695. I, Robert
> Pearson of Bishopfield in the parish of Allendale, being
> sick in body but of good and perfect memory doth
> bequeath my soul to Almighty God my creator and
> redeemer, and do make my last Will and Testament as
> followeth. I give unto my son Robert Pearson one bed-

stead, one table, all the pans, one iron pot, the iron bars, and the rest of the farm gear, and all my oxen gear, plows, and harrows. I give unto my sons Robert and Christopher Pearson equally betwixt them, all the rest my gear belonging unto husbandry. I give unto my son Christopher one bedstead in the loft, and wood to be a bed, and two farrows. I give unto my daughter Jane Wilson the bedstead where I now lie. I give unto my daughter Margaret Tallentire a panel chest. I give unto my son William Pearson one heifer. I give unto my granddaughter Ann Lowes a year-old heifer."

You can see the value of a will. It gives details of household items and farm equipment (other clauses concerning allocation of various farms and money came later), and, most important, it gives names of children, the married names of daughters, and the name of a granddaughter.

Another will we have seen gives some evidence of a family falling-out, because large sums of money (averaging 200 guineas) were left to each of several children, while at the end of these bequests were the words: "to my daughter, Jane Sharp, five shillings."

12 • Other Sources

In the previous chapters we talked about the principal sources of genealogical information. There are dozens of other records, of course, some well-known, others not. Some will be of help to you, some will not, but never assume any source is without value until you have checked it out. If the line of enquiry you have been following brings you to a dead-end, don't give up, don't assume there is no answer. Check back again with your original source, or try a totally different approach. Use your imagination, try far-out ideas, look for new sources. Here are some of them:

Passenger Lists: These have been kept from time to time in various countries. Don't expect a great deal of help from them as the odds are against you. Some do exist, of course, but the records of most people who crossed the Atlantic—after 1820— are to be found not in Europe but in the National Archives in Washington, D.C.

In the United Kingdom and Ireland only sporadic passenger lists were kept before 1890, and few passports were issued before 1914. When you consider the millions who fled from Ireland it is tragic to know that only a few thousand are recorded in Irish and UK sources.

In France there are more records, but you need to know the

name of the ship and, at least, the year of its sailing. They date from the early eighteenth century. One great asset is that they give the country of origin of the passenger, as many passengers through French ports came from other European countries. The lists for Le Havre (1750-1898) are in the Archives Départementales de la Seine Maritime, 76036 Rouen. There are similar records in Bordeaux (1713-1787) in the Archives Départementales de Gironde, 33000 Bordeaux.

In Germany, over five million emigrants who sailed from Hamburg are recorded. The records have been microfilmed by the LDS Church and are available through your nearest LDS branch library. You can also deal directly with the Museum für Hamburgische Geschichte, Holstenwall 24, 2000 Hamburg 36, West Germany. It will cost you more but you will receive an official certificate which will show name, age, occupation, names of children, and place of origin.

Several million people also sailed from the port of Bremen, but the authorities there destroyed the lists at intervals to make room for others. What they did not destroy themselves was destroyed by British bombing during World War II. An effort has been made to compile a list of certain passengers from Bremen who arrived in New York between 1847 and 1867, and these lists have been published by the Genealogical Publishing Company. The ports of Hamburg and Bremen were used extensively by emigrants from central and eastern Europe, so you do not need to be of German descent to find the lists and books of great value.

In Sweden there are no official passenger lists, but in the Landsarkivet at Göteborg you will find all the records and correspondence of the Larsson Brothers, emigration agents in that city. They give not only details of emigrants and their families, but also the names and addresses of relatives who had emigrated previously through the port. Passengers did not only come from Sweden and the other Scandinavian countries, but also from Germany and Russia.

In Belgium the archives in Antwerp (Het Rijksarchief

Antwerpen, Door Verstraeteplaats 2, 2000 Antwerpen) have records of passports issued in 1855 to emigrants. The registers have been copied and indexed by the LDS Church. The local archives (Stadsarchief Antwerpen) also have the hotel registers from 1679 to 1811 for foreigners, and from 1858 to 1898 for all nationalities. These lists can be valuable because many emigrants went to Antwerp to sail, only to find that sailing had been postponed. They then had to find a small hotel and a temporary job to tide them over until the new sailing date. In this port, as well as the others above, you will find emigrants from the Netherlands, France, and Germany, as well as from Belgium.

There are a few other scattered lists in Europe, as well as records of passports, and you will find fuller information in *In Search of Your European Roots.* Another helpful book— dealing more with arrival records than departure records—is Michael Tepper's *American Passenger Arrival Records* (Baltimore: Genealogical Publishing Company, 1988).

Military Records: If any of your ancestors from the United Kingdom and Ireland were regular soldiers, and you know the name of the regiment, you will probably find a good deal of information about them in the division of the Public Record Office located in Kew, Richmond, just outside London. The key to the information is the name of the regiment.

The records start in 1645 and the information you will get if your search is successful will be the soldier's home address, age, date of enlistment, name of wife and children, names of parents, details of wounds received, places in which he served, battles in which he was engaged, any pension or medals he was awarded, and—most interesting of all—a detailed physical description. For example —"Height 6 feet, weight 14 stone, hair black, complexion ruddy, eyes brown, wart on chin, 4-inch scar on left buttock, middle finger on left hand has tip missing." All this detail was to make him easier to catch if he deserted!

There were many desertions and do not think any the worse

of your ancestor if you find that he had deserted and received a hundred lashes. Conditions were appalling for the ordinary soldier. Many men joined with great reluctance because they and their family were starving and this was the only solution. In other cases, men were tricked into enlisting. A man who joined was given a shilling—known as the King's Shilling—and once he had taken it he was a soldier and could not change his mind. Recruiting sergeants would often tour the pubs and when they saw a likely lad they would try and enlist him. When he refused they would offer him a pint of beer, saying, "Well, no harm done, go your own way, but let's stand you a beer for friendship's sake." The unsuspecting man would drink the beer and as he drained the tankard a shilling would go into his mouth—slipped into his drink by the sergeant—and he would have taken the King's Shilling and become a soldier! No wonder there were so many desertions!

If you are of European descent you are even more likely to have a soldier in your ancestry because in most countries a period of military service was compulsory—sometimes a year, sometimes two years, followed by a period on the reserve. Many of these records are available in various archives and you will find them particularly in France, Germany, Switzerland, and in the areas originally within the Austro-Hungarian Empire.

Tombstones: Even though you know the date and location of grandfather's death, never miss a visit to the churchyard or burial ground and an inspection of the grave. If you cannot go yourself, try and get someone else to go. If all else fails write to the clergyman of the church, if grandfather was buried in a churchyard, or to the superintendent, if he was buried in a public burial ground. Why? Because there is often vital information on a tombstone which does not appear anywhere else. You may find his exact date and place of birth; information about his wife (if she is buried beside him) and her maiden name; details of children, perhaps some who died young and of whom you are unaware.

I know of one family in a village in Canada who learned the hard way about information in a churchyard. Their great-grandfather had been the original settler. They knew all about his background. He had arrived as a young man from Scotland, worked hard, raised a family, and died at a great age. He had been written about in local history books, and when he died there were lengthy obituaries in the local newspapers. His Scots descent was not in doubt. He had a Scots name and the family had inherited all sorts of Scots social customs. The only thing they didn't know was his exact place of birth. Oh, there were lots of stories. One branch of the family said he came from Perthshire, another insisted it was Ayrshire, and yet another was certain he came from Midlothian. A few years ago a family member started to trace the family back. He searched the available records of the LDS Church, he contacted the various genealogical organizations in Scotland, he went over there and searched through many church registers for the birth, and he traced down every lead and explored every by-way—all to no avail. Then he gave up the search and returned home. A few weeks later he went out for a walk—he still lived in the village where great-grandfather had settled—and his steps took him to the churchyard. He looked around for the grave—he hadn't bothered to look for it before; after all, they knew the exact date of his death, so what was the point? He eventually found the grave and the inscription was quite clear. There was great-grandfather's name, and that of his wife, and the dates of his birth and death. There was also one more line: "BORN IN INVERNESS, SCOTLAND."

When you are wandering round graveyards do have a look at some of the inscriptions. I have a couple of favorites. There is one in an old churchyard in Massachusetts which reads:

> Sacred to the memory of Jared Bates who departed this
> life 24 May 1834, aged 67 years. His wife Jane, aged 24,
> lives at 22 Elm St., and possesses every attribute for a
> good wife.

This is obviously an early commercial, and I hope it produced a good result for the lady! Another inscription I like very much I found in a cemetery in Essex, England, and it reads: "Here lie I, William Clarke, and I, his wife Janet, but quieter than we lay before."

Of course funny things can happen to the tombstones themselves. My great-grandfather, Robert Baxter, who died in 1890, is buried in the churchyard of the Priory Church in Lancaster, England. A few years ago I paid a return visit to the churchyard and found that Robert's plain, flat tombstone was no longer there. I searched for the sexton and asked what had happened. He explained that many of the tombstones had been moved because the grass around them could not be cut by a power mower, and it was no longer possible to find anyone who was prepared to use a hand mower. I asked, "What happened to them? Did you throw them out?" He replied, "Oh, no, sir, we could not do that. We've built an amphitheatre down the hill for open-air theatrical performances, and we used the tombstones for the seats."

So down the hill the two of us went and there was this beautiful amphitheatre cut into the hillside overlooking the River Lune, and in due course I found Robert's tombstone. I asked if this would give me free admission to all theatrical performances in future, and he took me very seriously and said, "Oh, no, sir, we couldn't do that. If we did it for thee we'd have to do it for everyone!" Poor great-grandfather Baxter lying in an unmarked grave, while the tourists sit on his tombstone and watch a play!

Often a tombstone may not be readable at all, or it may be readable only in a certain light at a certain angle. If you run into difficulties in deciphering the words, try taking photographs from several different angles. Oddly enough, by some trick of the light or the angle, a photograph often produces legible words. You may also find variations in the spelling of the surname on the same tombstone. We found a tombstone of my wife's Copland ancestors and on it the name was spelt Copeland and Coupland!

Quite often you will find that the clergyman of a church has in his possession a list of the tombstones in the churchyard, complete with the inscriptions. In many cases, too, a local archive or genealogical society has an indexed list of all the tombstone inscriptions in local cemeteries in the area.

Libraries: Be sure you check for information about your ancestors in the library of the place from whence they came and in the place where they settled. Libraries are no longer places where you only go to borrow a book. More and more, they are developing into local archives. They have histories of early settlers and of the local area. You may find a lot of information about your family in such books. In addition, they have unpublished manuscripts on the same subjects. A local historian may have spent years researching a local history in the hope it would be published. Unfortunately, publishers will not produce such a book unless they can be sure it will sell at least 5,000 copies, so the author abandons the idea and gives the library his precious manuscript.

Let me tell you a story which illustrates this kind of occurrence. Some years ago my wife and I decided to research her Copland ancestors. We knew they came from the valley of the River Nith, near a town named Dumfries, in the south-west of Scotland. We went to Dumfries and the first thing we did was to go into the local library and see the librarian. We asked, "Do you happen to have anything about a family named Copland who were prominent in this area in the last century?" "Oh, yes," he replied, "we certainly do," and off he went, coming back with a 250-page history of the Copland family! It had been written fifty years before by a member of the family quite unknown to us. It had been carefully researched, giving details of all his sources of information, and covered a period back to 1135 in an unbroken line to a man named Ulf the Viking, Lord of Copeland. My wife knew her ancestry back for five generations and we were able to fit her branch into the family tree without any difficulty. Just by going into the library we had saved ourselves a great deal of time and money!

There was an exciting sequel to this. From the information in the manuscript we traced the widow of a very distant cousin hitherto unknown to us. She had a number of fascinating Copland family possessions since her late husband had been descended from the senior branch of the family. These included a sixteenth-century quaich (now in the Victoria and Albert Museum), a very rare and very valuable "breeches" Bible, and several old tablecloths in perfect condition. She was kind enough to give my wife a damask one, specially woven for the marriage of Alexander Copland and Anne Gordon in 1735. Woven into the material was the date, the names of the bride and groom, their coats-of-arms. It was used at the wedding feast and had been so used for every Copland wedding since then. With it was an enormous napkin also specially woven for the great occasion. We used them at the wedding reception after the marriage of our daughter, and so the tradition was continued, and no doubt they will be used by our granddaughter if, or when, she marries. It is a priceless possession and is an example of the kind of unknown treasure you, too, may discover on your magic journey into the past of your family! All this from a visit to a library one day in Scotland!

Genealogical Societies: All over North America, Europe, Australia, and New Zealand there are hundreds of genealogical societies or family history societies. It will pay you to find out if one exists in the area from which your family came in the old country as well as in the area in this country in which your immigrant ancestor settled. If there is one where you live, you should certainly join. Regular meetings are held and if you join one you will find dozens of people who are tracing their ancestors, and you will learn a great deal both from the members themselves and from the speakers at their meetings. Ancestor-hunting can sometimes be a lonely affair if no family members are interested in what you are doing, and by joining your local genealogical organization you will immediately realize you are not alone in your search.

The advantage of joining an organization overseas is that you will receive a regular newsletter telling you of new records which have been discovered in the area, or old records which have just been made available for public search. You will be able to find out if some unknown distant cousin is a member and is researching your family. You will be able—usually for free—to put a query in the newsletter which may help to solve a problem for you. You may be able to help someone else in the world who has a problem.

An example for you. I belong to the Cumbria Family History Society, in England. This covers the area of the old counties of Cumberland and Westmorland, now merged in the new county of Cumbria, together with parts of Lancashire and Yorkshire (you will find out about the changes in counties in England and Wales in the next chapter). A couple of years ago I saw a query in the newsletter. It was from a William Baxter, in Australia, who was descended from a Joseph Baxter, born in Morecambe, Lancashire, in 1804. He asked if anyone had information about him and his ancestors. I had a record of him. He was a cousin of my great-great-grandfather and I was able to send William Baxter a complete family tree which took him back to 1340! He was rather pleased!

Newspapers: Don't neglect newspapers as a source of information. Many libraries in this country have projects of abstracting the names of people mentioned in the issues of the local newspaper, giving each individual mentioned an index card with details as to why his name appeared in the paper—obituary, marriage, birth or baptism, tribute, vote of thanks, election to office, wife-beating, drunk and disorderly, assault, etc. So this is another reason to check with libraries.

Don't hesitate to write a letter to a newspaper asking for the help of readers in finding out about your family. Big-city newspapers are unlikely to publish such a letter, but small-town newspapers usually do because it is news for its local readership. Keep your letter as short as possible. A couple of years back a woman spoke to me after one of my lectures and said, "My grandfather, George Stevens, emigrated from the county of Suffolk in 1865. I don't know where in the county he was born. What can I do, because it's a common name?" I suggested she write to the Editor, The Daily Newspaper, Ipswich (that's the county town of Suffolk) on the following lines: "My grandfather, George Stevens, emigrated from Suffolk in 1865. He left brothers and sisters behind. If there are any descendants of them still in the area I would very much like to hear from them." I asked her to let me know how she got on, and a few months later she wrote to tell me that she had four replies from second and third cousins, and one of them was a keen genealogist who had already traced the family back in Suffolk for 200 years!

At this point you may be saying, "My great-grandfather emigrated in 1835—how could anyone over there know anything about him after a century and a half?" You are very probably wrong. You must realize that when your great-grandfather emigrated it was the most appalling and dramatic event the family had ever known. A son or a brother was leaving home forever to go across the ocean to a distant country, never to return or to be seen again! It was unforgettable within the family, and the memory of it was often referred to in conversation. Whenever this country is mentioned in the news, some present-day member of the family is likely to say, "Do you remember the story about great-grandfather's brother emigrating there in the last century? I wonder whatever happened to him? Maybe we have lots of relatives over there." They won't make any attempt to find you, but if your letter appears you are very likely to hear from them.

In my early days of ancestor-hunting I wrote to several local newspapers in this way, obtaining good results and much vital information as a result.

As a matter of fact, I wrote a letter quite recently to a newspaper in the Lake District of England. I knew it circulated in the area from which my family came and where they had farmed and raised sheep for 600 years. I had very few photographs of the valley and the eight or nine farms which the Baxters had owned over the centuries, so I wrote and asked if any of the readers had any photographs of the farms (I named them) and if so, whether they could have them copied at my expense. Three people, quite unknown to each other, went to great trouble to make a special visit to the remote valley and take photographs. One couple took fifty feet of movie film and lots of stills; two ladies made a tour of the valley by car, taking photographs at frequent intervals, mounted them in the right order in an album and sent it to me; and a man discovered the ruins of a house at the very head of the valley beyond the end of the lane and a quarter of a mile beyond the last farm. It dated back to about 1300 and I am still trying to find out if it was a Baxter house! All this proves how kind and helpful people are and the lengths to which they will go to be of assistance.

•   •   •

There are still more records which I will name and not describe, but you will find full details in my books. There are land records, apprenticeship lists, court records, tithe payment lists, tax records, marriage licenses, school attendance records, etc. There are also estate papers—these are the detailed records of the great landed estates of the aristocracy of a country which have been handed over to archives and record offices. If your grandfather was a plowman on the estate of the Earl of Lonsdale, you will probably find out a good deal about him and his family among the Lowther Papers in the County Record Office in Carlisle. If your grandmother was a nursemaid on the estate of the Von Bülow family of Gross-Brunsrode in Nieder-Sachsen, West Germany, you will find the records in the archives of that state. If grandfather was a skilled craftsman working for the Carl Zeiss Company in Jena, you will find his personnel records in a special company museum.

If you are tracing ancestors in Scotland there are two things to bear in mind. First, you have to know about the Register of

Sasines in the Scottish Record Office. The word sasine comes from "seize." To be seized of land meant to possess it. There is no such thing as "a sasine." Taking sasine was the ceremony by which a man became the legal owner of a piece of land. It entailed the handing over on the land itself of earth and stone by the seller to the buyer. The sasine records contain a great deal of information about other members of the family. In my wife's Pearson family we had failed for a long time to find the surname of the wife of a certain man. We knew she was named Margaret, but that was all. When we traced the record of sasine for the sale of some land after his death we found her original surname mentioned.

The second thing to remember in Scotland is hand-festing. This was a simple ceremony between a man and woman in which they held hands, the groom said, "I take you, Margaret Spence, to be my wedded wife," and the bride replied, "I take you, James Wilson, to be my wedded husband." These declarations had to be made over water—so it always took place on a bridge over a river or a burn—in the presence of witnesses. This was quite legal and binding. However, the church authorities and the local minister did not like it, and pressure was always brought to bear on the couple to have a wedding in the kirk. There were threats of hellfire and damnation, the couple were ostracized by their neighbors, and so they usually gave in after awhile and had their kirk wedding. However, there were always the strong-minded or awkward people who refused to conform and proceeded to produce children on an almost annual basis. The children were refused baptism in many parishes and this increased the social and religious pressure so that, after perhaps eight years, they gave in and had a religious wedding in the kirk. So you may find the marriage of an ancestor on a certain date and then see that his eight children were all baptized at the same time!

13 • County Record Offices

This chapter is primarily for people whose ancestors came from England and Wales, since other parts of Great Britain and Ireland do not have such valuable archives. Although a few counties have had record offices since before World War II, not many were established before the great changes in county boundaries in 1974 and the simultaneous outburst of interest in ancestor-hunting.

The two smallest counties in England (the Isle of Ely and Rutland) disappeared, and so did Cumberland, Huntingdon, Middlesex, and Westmorland. With most of the other counties that remained there were boundary changes—some minor, such as the transfer of territory from Suffolk to Norfolk, and some major, like the division of Yorkshire into five new counties. The only counties whose boundaries remained unchanged were Bedfordshire, Cornwall, Essex, Hertfordshire, Isle of Wight, Kent, Northamptonshire, Shropshire (Salop), and Wiltshire.

The changes in boundaries also meant a massive transfer of records from one county to another. This led to the establishment of County Record Offices in practically all counties in England and Wales in order to accommodate the masses of material being transferred. The CROs, of course, contain all kinds of official county records as well as items of vital importance to ancestor-hunters.

Before you start searching for records in England and Wales it is essential that you familiarize yourself with all the new boundaries (refer to *In Search of Your British and Irish Roots*). You can no longer say, "Grandfather came from Yorkshire. Let's go over to England and look at the records in the County Record Office." Which county? Which office? Which city? It could be Beverley, Middlesbrough, Northallerton, Sheffield, or Wakefield! The old county of Yorkshire is now split up into Cleveland, Humberside, North Yorkshire, South Yorkshire, and West Yorkshire. There is homework to be done and knowledge to be acquired before you visit or write to England and Wales.

The County Record Offices come under the authority of the County Council and are each headed by a County Archivist. Their genealogical records include almost everything—except tombstones—which you will need for research in a particular county. The co-operation you will receive from a county archivist and his staff varies from enthusiastic co-operation over and above the call of duty, to reluctant assistance. A lot depends on you, too, and your approach. Remember that some CROs operate on a shoestring, while others are most generously funded. So when you make an enquiry write a nice letter, cover the return postage, and offer to pay whatever fees are required.

Generally speaking the CROs will make a simple search for you for free, or for a very small fee. If your enquiry is more complicated they will tell you they do not have the staff available, and will enclose a list of professional researchers or record agents with whom you can make your own financial arrangements. What is a "simple" enquiry and what is a "complicated" one? Let me give you examples. A simple one would be: "Can you please check the 1871 census return and give me details of an entry for a family named Williamson (the head of the family was a Thomas Williamson) living at a farm called Netherwood in the village of Dunham?" A complicated enquiry might be: "Can you check the parish registers of Dunham for the name Williamson and list the names of any people with that surname who appeared in the registers of baptism, marriage, and death between 1750 and 1841?"

What sort of records will you find in a CRO? This cannot be answered with absolute accuracy because there is variation from county to county. In my book mentioned above I list the records available in each CRO. However, let us take the county of Suffolk as a fairly typical example. Its records include the following items: parish registers, census returns, wills, court records, Bishops' Transcripts, Nonconformist registers, marriage licenses, tithes paid, marriage indexes, churchyard inscriptions, pedigrees, biographies, directories, and early newspapers.

If you are planning a visit to the old country and intend to visit a CRO and do your own searching, remember that you are only one of many thousands doing this, and many CROs have very limited space available for researchers. When your vacation plans are made write to the CRO and book a table for the particular day you will be there, otherwise you may be turned away at the door and also discover that all space is reserved for several weeks ahead.

If your ancestors were Welsh you will need to know about the new county boundaries because the changes have been quite drastic. Instead of thirteen counties you now have eight. Two other problems exist for you in that country. First—particularly in the north and west—you will find Welsh is a living language. You may find some of the records you need are written in this language and not in English. Second, Wales was a hotbed of Nonconformity, and John Wesley's Methodism and all its many sects flourished. You will find details of the various religions and sects later in this book.

The other major result of the establishment of new counties and County Record Offices was the formation of a family history society in each county in England and Wales. Working closely with the CROs, the societies have played a major part in solving many of the problems of ancestor-hunters. If you know the county from which your ancestors came, it will be worth-while to join.

You will notice I have been talking only about England and Wales. There have been no county boundary changes in Scotland or Ireland. In Scotland there are only a few family history societies—located in Aberdeen, Glasgow, Dundee, Inverness, and Hawick. Because Scotland is such a small country you will find that almost every record you need is in Edinburgh. In Northern Ireland there is one family history society in Belfast; in Eire the Irish Family History Society is located in County Offaly. There are also family history societies in the Isle of Man and the Channel Islands.

For up-to-date information about addresses of the secretaries of all the family history societies in the UK and Ireland I suggest you write to the Secretary, Federation of Family History Societies, c/o Benson Room, Birmingham and Midland Institute, Margaret Street, Birmingham B3 3BS, enclosing *three* International Reply Coupons and a self-addressed airmail envelope. Without these enclosures you will not get a reply!

I cannot attempt to list county boundary changes and family history societies in all the European countries. For that information you will have to refer to my book *In Search of Your European Roots,* in which all this information is listed in great detail.

14 • Religion

In this chapter I want to talk about religion—not to have a theological argument setting one religion against another, but to explain some problems in religious customs and organizations which may make life difficult for you. Do not jump to any conclusions about the religion of your ancestors as you trace back in different countries. Remember that people can change religions for several reasons. Your immediate family may be Lutheran or Catholic or Presbyterian—two or three generations back they could have been Baptists.

Religions can change because of marriage, because of conviction and conversion, or because of necessity. Your immigrant ancestor may have been staunch Church of England, and his forbears before him. He arrived in this country and went into an area of new settlement. He found there was no Anglican or Episcopal church there, but there was a Methodist circuit rider who came round every three months and held a service in someone's house, baptized children, married people, and held a funeral service by the grave of someone who had died since his last visit. Would your ancestor have stopped going to church because there was only a Methodist minister in the area occasionally? I doubt it. He would have accepted what he might have regarded as second best. When a church of his own denomination was eventually built he might have returned to

77

his original faith, or by then his ties to the Methodist Church may have been so strong that he never did. Bear this sort of thing in mind if you fail to find an ancestor listed in the records of what you regard as your family religion.

Another problem you will encounter is caused by the fact that in a number of countries marriages were not regarded as legal unless they took place in a parish church of the official state religion. In England and Wales, for example, up to 1753 Catholics, Quakers, Jews, and Nonconformists in general could be married in their own churches, chapels, meeting houses, or synagogues. After 1753 all marriages (except for Quakers and Jews) had to take place in the parish churches of the Church of England. By 1837 these restrictions were no longer in force, but during this period you must be prepared to check the Church of England registers even though your ancestors did not belong to that church. If your ancestors were Baptists you should also remember that in that religion children were not baptized until they had reached the age of reason, and adults were baptized if they joined the church late in life. In Baptist registers, therefore, you will find records of people being baptized between the ages of nine and ninety or thereabouts.

The Methodist movement began in 1738 when John and Charles Wesley—both Church of England clergymen—set out to inspire a greater sense of spirituality and holiness in the established church and its doctrines. They were joined by George Whitefield, a friend of the brothers when they were all at Oxford University. Whitefield set up tabernacles for the meetings of his own followers, and the Wesleys established preaching houses. In 1741 Whitefield split away from the Wesleys—the first of the innumerable schisms in the Nonconformist movement. By 1784 Methodist ministers were barred from Church of England churches, but their children were still baptized in the established churches since this was recognized as legal, whereas baptisms in their own chapels were not.

In the years which followed, the succession of splits led to such sects as New Connection, Independent Methodists, Primitive Methodists, Bible Christians, Protestant Methodists, United Churches of Christ, Regular Methodists, United Methodists, Calvinists, Lady Huntingdon's Connection, True Methodists, and Wesleyan Methodists.

Even the Quakers split into Inghamites, Hicksites, True Believers, and Fast Friends. (The register books kept by the Society of Friends (Quakers) record births, marriages, and burials. Baptism was not practiced.) The Baptists, too, were not immune from schisms. There were General Baptists, Particular Baptists, Strict Baptists, Seventh-Day Baptists, the Old Baptist Union, and the Churches of Christ. The Unitarian Church also originated within the Baptist movement.

Most of the Nonconformist churches were totally independent of all other churches or chapels within their particular sect. There was no central governing body—only a very loose association of fiercely individualistic religious meeting places. Many of the smaller sects did not even possess their own chapel but met in different houses under the leadership of a lay preacher elected from within the group. This is why so many Nonconformist records have disappeared and why you will have more problems tracing your dissenting ancestors than if you were of solid Church of England descent. If you are tracing Methodist or Baptist ancestors in a particular area or city, be sure you check the registers of all the different sects operating there at that time. So far as Methodist records are concerned, bear in mind that the chapels were often part of a circuit round which a minister travelled holding services in a number of different locations. A register under the name of a place called Frampton may include a dozen different villages around Frampton and not merely the place named in the title.

In Scotland there were not the same divisions. The Presbyterian Church, although consisting of an association of independent churches, was much more unified. Only one split occurred in its ranks—when the Free Presbyterian Church broke away from the mainstream. It never became a major force, however, and was known in Scotland as "The Wee Frees."

So far as Wales is concerned, Nonconformity was very strong indeed. Calvinistic Methodism was the mainstream, but it had many brooks and rivulets both within and without the hardcore center. There were Societies, Bands, and Classes, and in a small village there could be several different sects—each of which would be convinced that it was the true guide to eventual salvation. The moderate section of the Calvinistic Methodists was nominally part of the Church of England until 1811, but the relationship was a tenuous one, and many of the sects had been splitting away since the mid-1700s. I suppose those characteristics—independence, free-thinking, strength of character, orneriness—which made them question the tenets of the old religion made them hard to get along with in the new one.

The Civil Registration Act of 1837 took away the legal basis for the recording of vital events by the various religions and placed the responsibility on the government through district registry offices. The Nonconformist churches and chapels in England and Wales were told to give up registers up to that date, and these are now in the Public Record Office in London, in Chancery Lane. Some Welsh registers were not deposited (that awkwardness again!), but most of these are now in the National Library of Wales at Aberystwyth, or in the various CROs. Many of the CROs in both England and Wales now have copies of the various Nonconformist registers for the county on microfilm.

The general policy of the Catholic Church is to leave the original registers in the original churches, but some dioceses have microfilmed them for their own archives, and in a very few cases the original registers have been handed over to the CROs.

Many of the above remarks apply to some of the European countries, but there were not nearly as many divisions within the churches. The Protestants (Huguenots) in France went through several periods of persecution, and many thousands fled the country to England, Germany, and the Netherlands and established their own churches. There are many records of these congregations, and there are details of the various locations in two of my books—the one about Great Britain and Ireland, and the other about Europe.

The Lutheran Church is strong in Scandinavia, Germany, the Netherlands, and Austria. The Catholic Church, of course, is the predominant religion in France, Spain, Portugal, and Italy, with a very strong following in the Netherlands. In the latter country at various times in the sixteenth and seventeenth centuries Catholics, Jews, Mennonites, and others were compelled to have their children baptized and married in a Dutch Reformed church—this being the state religion at the time.

One unique problem exists in what is now Germany. Before 1871 the country did not exist; instead, it was a collection of kingdoms, grand duchies, electorates, principalities, and dukedoms. In some of these areas the inhabitants were compelled to adopt the religion of the ruler, and when the ruler changed by death or conquest, so did the religion of the people!

15 • The Family Tree

Now that you have started tracing your ancestors you begin to grow your family tree. There are several different ways of designing a family tree but a great deal depends on just what and who you want to record. I have seen some very artsy-craftsy and complicated ones which consist of a drawing of a large tree with dozens of branches stretching out in all directions, each bearing the name of a family member, and each branch sprouting twigs of various lengths with more names inscribed. I have seen other ones which end up on a great roll of paper four feet wide and fifty feet long which stretches from the front door to the back and halfway down the garden path.

It really all depends on you. Obviously you have been keeping all the basic information in notebooks, written down immediately as you obtain it, together with a note of the name of the person from whom you obtained it. There are a variety of printed forms which you can buy from any genealogical society. Some provide space for eight generations back on four sides of your family, or as many as eight or sixteen. Perhaps you will want something like this, but what is your aim in tracing back? Do you simply want to trace all your living relatives on all sides, including the most distant cousins? If this is what you want there are no printed forms which will be suitable. I know a woman in New York whose only interest is in living relatives.

She already knows over 300 of them and each of them has a page in three 3-ring binders.

My own system is a little different, but it works very well for me. I have a notebook for each family in my ancestry which I have traced. This happens to be three on my mother's side (Cantle, Burley, Parsons) and two on my father's (Baxter and Caley). The notebooks contain all the information I have found, including information on several distant cousins. I also have a family tree for each, framed and on the wall of my study. These are quite small—13″ x 11″— but they contain all the information I want to display going back for as much as 400 years. (The only exception is the Baxter family which is larger because it goes back for 600 years.) In each case I show the direct line of descent to me, but all the brothers and sisters of my grandfather, great-grandfather, and so on are listed together on the right side of the tree. In this way several generations can be shown in quite a small space. I will show you on the next page my Cantle family tree so that you can understand how simple the system is:

John Cantel (married Alice—surname unknown).
Died in Keynsham, Somerset, 1643.

William	Cecilie
Born 1639 Keynsham	Marie
= Elizabeth (surname unknown)	Anne

Edward	Elizabeth	Mary
Born 1674 Keynsham	Robert	George
Died 1766 Keynsham	Elinor	Sarah
= (1) Mary. Died 1715	Mary	Sarah
= (2) Elizabeth Cadham in 1716		

(1) James	(2) **Job**	Esther	Edward
Sara	Born Keynsham	Betty	George
Ann	1717	John	
	= Sarah Balme		
	in 1751		

Job Cantle	Sarah	Thomas
Born 1757 Keynsham	Mary	Anne
= Betty Hale		

George	Ann	Job
Born 1795 Keynsham	James	Joseph
= Elizabeth Charlton	David	Thomas

Henry	Thomas
Born 1815 Keynsham	
= Alice Wood	

George	Frederick	Walter
Born 1840 Keynsham	Elizabeth	Emily
= Elizabeth Parsons in 1862		

Joyce	Elizabeth	Henry
Born 1880 Bristol	Elizabeth	Alice
= William Baxter	George	Frank
1906 Bristol	Walter	Florence
Died 1959 Edinburgh	Wilbert	Ernest
	Sidney	

Angus Baxter

There are several comments to make about this particular family tree which may be helpful:

(1) All the information about the first eight generations was obtained from the parish registers of the village of Keynsham, Somerset. At the time, the registers had not been copied by the LDS Church, and so I wrote to the rector and asked if he could arrange for someone to copy all the Cantle entries in the register from the earliest date up to 1850. (I already knew the family had originated in Keynsham and had all the necessary information since that date.) The rector told me he had found someone reliable who would do the copying. He told me it would cost $25. I sent him the money and in due course the list of names and dates arrived. Because the family had been farmers in the area continuously from the early 1600s and had never left it, I was able to sit down with the list and complete the family tree as you see it.

(2) There are missing dates at times and, probably, if I wished, I could trace more information from some of the other records I mentioned earlier in this book. However, as it stands, it gives me my direct ancestral descent on my mother's side from 1639 to the present day, and that was the main purpose of the search.

(3) You will notice on two occasions in the lists of brothers and sisters of my direct ancestor (shown on the right) there is a duplication of names—in the third generation two Sarahs and in the ninth two Elizabeths. This is because the first child had died and the name given to her was repeated when the next child arrived. This happened very often because of frequent infant mortality and the need (or custom) of a naming pattern. Up until the later years of the last century the eldest son was named after the father's father, the second son after the mother's father, the third son after the father; the eldest daughter after the mother's mother, the second daughter after the father's mother, the third daughter after the mother. There were exceptions to the naming pattern when it produced a duplication of names. In that case the name was taken from the

next on the list, i.e., if the eldest son was named John after the father's father, and the mother's father was also a John, then the second son could not be named after him, and was therefore named after the father.

Another break in the pattern could be caused by death, as I showed above with the Sarahs and Elizabeths. Nowadays, people who lose a child are not inclined to use the same name for a subsequent child, but this is a comparatively recent development. I have known a case where five successive sons were named John because each one died in turn. That is why it is always wise to check the deaths or burials when you are checking the births or baptisms—often a child would die within a few days or weeks of birth.

(4) You will notice in the third generation that Edward married twice. In such a case you make clear which children are descended from which mother by the numbers (1) and (2) as I have done above.

(5) So far as the brothers and sisters of my direct ancestor are concerned I do not show in the family tree any details of their birth, marriage, death, or their children. I have all this information on file, but it is not of major interest to me and so I do not clutter up the tree with unnecessary branches. My primary concern is *my* direct descent.

One unsolved mystery in the history of my Cantle ancestors is their origin. According to my mother there was a family story that they had originated in France. The original Cantle shown above (John) was in Keynsham when his first child was born in 1639, but where did he come from? His daughters all had first names which could have been French. His own name could have been anglicized from Jean. He could have been a Huguenot refugee but the dates make it unlikely. On the other hand, in Old English, or Anglo-Saxon, the word cantle means a point of land, so he could just as easily have been descended from someone known as William of the cantle, or John of the cantle, or whomever! Perhaps one day when I am no longer writing or lecturing or answering my heavy mail I may have the time to really investigate the true origins of the family.

If you are going to frame and display your family tree, it can be typed, or you can get an heraldic artist or an expert calligrapher to produce a very attractive one at no major expense.

There is one other attractive possibility. If you have traced back your family on one side and also your husband or wife's family on one side, you can set out the two trees side by side, each generation of one family level with the same generation of the other, and end with your name at the bottom of one tree and your spouse's at the bottom of the other, and the two names joined with the marriage sign (=) and then your children set out below:

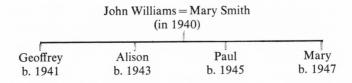

John Williams = Mary Smith
(in 1940)

Geoffrey	Alison	Paul	Mary
b. 1941	b. 1943	b. 1945	b. 1947

Be sure you leave space below for the addition of your descendants as they come along!

16 • Jewish Sources

Many people of Jewish descent are convinced of the absolute impossibility of tracing their ancestry. Of course, there are problems which do not exist for Gentiles, but most of them can be overcome. It is impossible to do justice to this subject in a short chapter, and for a detailed explanation of Jewish sources I must refer you to my books mentioned earlier, as each of them has a special section devoted to Jewish records. All I can do here is to talk to you in general terms.

The Jews of Europe were divided into two main groups: those living in Spain and Portugal were Sephardim (a medieval Hebrew word meaning Spaniard) and all the others Ashkenazim (Germans). The latter lived in the Rhine Valley and, later, in Russia and Poland, and in eastern Europe generally.

There are three factors which must remain uppermost in your mind at all times as you search for your Jewish ancestors: (1) the records you will need are not necessarily to be found in Jewish archives; (2) every year new sources of information are being found; and (3) you will have problems with family names. Often names were simplified or anglicized—Kanofsky became Kane, Moses became Morris, Martinez became Martin, and so on. Another complication is the literal translation of a name. For instance, Zevi in Hebrew became Hart in English and Hirsch in German. Until the eighteenth and nineteenth centuries in Europe many Jews did not have a family name. They had lived in isolated settlements, or ghettos, and there was not the pressing need for a surname. "Moses, son of Aaron" was a quite sufficient description for recognition in a small, tightly-knit community. In some cases—particularly among the Sephardim—family names based on occupations did start to develop in Europe in the seventeenth century, but they were often only used within the family and had no legal validity.

In the eighteenth and nineteenth centuries many European countries passed laws compelling Jews to adopt family names. When they had to make such a choice it was often based on a wide variety of facts or fancies. Of course the most popular choice was that of occupation, so a tailor became Snider, a carpenter Nagel, and so on. And there were other choices—a small man was Klein, a short one Kurtz, a religious man Gottlieb, a man from the east Osterman. In certain areas, such as the northwest of what is now Germany, the name Rose was very popular, and in these districts there were many variations of this—Rosen, Rosenkrantz, Rosenbloom, Rosengarten, Rosenthal, etc.

There were other factors in the choice of a surname. In Frankfurt, for example, houses were distinguished by signs instead of numbers, so very many Jews took names based on the sign of their house. Someone living in a house with a red shield became Rothschild, or if the sign was a ship the name became Schiff.

In England in the seventeenth century it was quite common for a Portuguese or Spanish Jew to use an alias, or several aliases, to protect his relatives still living in the Iberian Peninsula. Let me give you an actual example from English records. Isaac Heim Pereira was known outside the synagogue as Manoel Lopes Pereira, but in business he was also called Manuel de Velasquez and Jacques Vendepeere. These various names appear in his will in 1709.

Records of English Jewry go back a long way, but the registers are not always easy to follow as they were written in

Hebrew, or in Yiddish in a Hebrew script. In addition, the names recorded do not always correspond to the names used outside the synagogue. Often no surname is given, and in other cases the name used in the registers was obviously a nick-name. How else can you explain "Hayim ben Eleazar Grey-hound"? That name appears in a seat-holders' list of the Great Synagogue of London in 1766.

England: The first Jews arrived here with William the Conqueror in 1066. From then onwards there were commu-nities of French-speaking Jews in many of the main towns. They were expelled in 1290 but started to return two centuries later. By the early sixteenth century some 200 had again settled in the country. Their stay was a short one: when a Jewish leader was executed they left England once again and did not return until about 1550.

The first Jews to settle were Sephardic Jews from Portugal, and there was a steady stream of immigrants between 1550 and 1760. The main settlements were in London and Bristol, with the great majority living in the capital—over 2,000 by 1680. The first synagogue there was established in 1656 and in 1701 the congregation moved to a new building on Bevis Marks at Hineage Lane. The congregation still worships at this syna-gogue, and all its records are in the building next door. The entries are in Portuguese until 1819. The surnames are indexed under births, marriages, and deaths. By 1690 the first Ash-kenazim synagogue was established in London.

It was not easy for the Jews to become established in Eng-land—many occupations were closed to them because of the anti-Semitic guild system which prevented Jews joining a craft guild. However, they spread across the country as peddlers, tailors, glassworkers, jewellers, etc. By the early part of the nineteenth century there were at least thirteen congregations outside London.

A great many records exist in the original synagogues and also in the Jewish Museum and the United Synagogue

Archives. Remember, too, that Jews had to participate in civil registration (from 1837), census enumeration, and so on. Many Jewish families practiced their faith in secret and, for this reason, were baptized, married, and buried in the local church.

Europe: In most European countries the Jewish people were required to register vital events in the local state church—Catholic or Protestant.

The most complete Jewish records are found in Austria, France, Germany, and Italy, whereas those from Eastern Europe are more fragmentary. The reasons for the latter condition are obvious—the pogroms and the diaspora. However, there are many Jewish organizations in the United States which now have many records from the East, and all of them are listed in my *In Search of Your European Roots.*

All things are possible and with reasonable good fortune you should be able to trace your Jewish ancestors in Europe for at least 200 years—probably further back in some Western countries and in England.

17 • Coats-of-Arms

Let me say at once that there is little chance that you or your family have any right to a coat-of-arms. You may have seen a store in some shopping center displaying "family" coats-of-arms, or received a circular letter from some company offering you a copy of your "family" coat-of-arms. You may even have had an offer of a whole dinner-service with your coat-of-arms, or a tastefully designed shield to hang in your toilet, or wherever. There are coats-of-arms book matches, lampshades, wine glasses, notepaper, bookplates, bookmarks, silverware, tankards, decals, flags, pennants, and a host of other items with useless decorations. It is big business, but it has no basis in fact, and no connection with your quest for your ancestors. Do not be separated from your money.

How the scheme works is simple. Let us say your name is Adamson and you are unwise enough to spend your money on one of the gee-jaws I have mentioned. You will receive an Adamson coat-of-arms, all right, but it will not be *your* coat-of-arms. So far as the United Kingdom or any European country is concerned, the right to a coat-of-arms was originally granted by the head of state to a particular individual "and his heirs in the direct male line." This means that this person and his sons and grandsons, and so on, were the only ones with a legal right to use a particular coat-of-arms.

So far as you are concerned, you will have received a copy of a coat-of-arms granted at some time in history to a man named Adamson. He could have been a man who owned vast estates in Scotland in the Middle Ages, or he could have been a man who "bought" a knighthood by contributing large sums of money to a particular political party when it was in power. It could also be a complete invention of the company selling the product.

I know a particular lady—let's call her Miss Laidlaw, though that bears no resemblance to her name—who answered one of these advertisements which appear in magazines near the truss ads. She sent off $25 and in due course received a beautifully varnished small wooden shield with a coat-of-arms on it below the magic words "THE LAIDLAW FAMILY." She was delighted with it and it was duly hung on the wall in the living room. She then wrote and told her two brothers about it—one lived in California and the other in British Columbia. They, too, sent off their hard-earned $25 and each of them received a varnished shield with the Laidlaw family coat-of-arms. There was only one drawback—they ended up with three totally different coats-of-arms between them!

Remember that back over the centuries the ruler of a country granted the right to a coat-of-arms to a man who had done him some service—lent him money, raised a troop of soldiers to fight for him, procured ladies for the royal bed, or even just made him laugh. The odds are that your ancestors and mine were far too low on the social scale to have ever even met the ruler, much less having done him or her a service. They were farmers or merchants or peasants. They were fishermen, thatchers, shepherds, plowmen, stonemasons, gamekeepers, soldiers, priests, ostlers, tavern-keepers, or any one of a thousand different occupations fairly low on the social scale; they were not on visiting terms with kings and queens. They never had coats-of-arms.

Although grants of arms are still made in England and Scotland, it was in the Middle Ages that most coats-of-arms were first recorded. How did it all start?

The historian Herodotus, writing 400 years before Christ, said, "The Carians seem to be the first who put crests upon their helmets and sculptured devices upon their shields." Caria was in Asia Minor, on what is now the Mediterranean coast of Turkey. From that time on there were many references to shields and ornamental devices. Once a man had a shield to use in battle it was a logical development for him to decorate it so it was recognizable, and thus other men would be able to identify the mighty warrior from afar.

In the Middle Ages everyone fought—the knight because knights were expected to fight or because he owed allegiance to his king, or because he wanted the estates of his next-door neighbor, or even his next-door neighbor's delightful daughter. The ordinary man fought because the knight owned him and told him what to do. The knight's men-at-arms then started to wear a linen surcoat over their chain-mail armor. Originally it was to stop the armor getting wet and rusty in damp climates or too hot in hot climates. The next step was to decorate the surcoat with a symbol so that each man knew who was for him and who was against him. Usually the symbol was that of the knight or earl or king who owned the soldiers. Thus the surcoat became known as the coat-of-arms.

Of course there were not many knights, and even fewer barons, and the right to a coat-of arms was restricted to a very tiny segment of the population in the Middle Ages. It was not until the early seventeenth century that grants of arms were given more generously, and wealthy businessmen received them —plus a title. Because such a small percentage of the population had a right to a coat-of-arms, it follows that only a few people alive today have inherited that right.

However, it may be that you will discover a genuine family coat-of-arms, and this chapter will tell you what it is, how you find it, and what you do with it.

In England, the approval of coats-of-arms and, if necessary, the proving of the right to them, is the responsibility of the College of Arms in London. This is headed by the Earl Marshal of England, a hereditary title always borne by the Duke of Norfolk. He is assisted by three Kings-of-Arms— Garter, Norroy, and Clarenceux. Garter is the principal King-of-Arms and is the deputy of the Earl Marshal. Norroy is responsible for that part of the country north of the River Trent and Clarenceux for everything to the south of it.

There are six Heralds—Chester, Windsor, Lancaster, York, Richmond, and Somerset. There are four Pursuivants— Rouge-Croix, Blue-Mantle, Rouge-Dragon, and Portcullis. Rouge-Croix is named from the red cross of St. George in the arms of England, Blue-Mantle from the blue mantle of France assumed by Edward III, Rouge-Dragon from the arms of Wales, and Portcullis from the badge of Henry VII.

In Scotland, the equivalent of the Earl Marshal is the Lyon King-of-Arms, known as the Lord Lyon, or simply as "The Lyon." (I visited him a few years ago, and when his secretary said, "The Lyon is waiting for you now," I felt like an early Christian in an arena in Rome!) His office is not hereditary and the appointment is made by the Crown. There are three Scottish Heralds—Ross, Rothesay, and Albany—and three Pursuivants —Unicorn, Falkland, and Carrick.

The Office of Arms in Ireland is headed by the Ulster King-of-Arms. Under him is a Pursuivant named Athlone. There are also two Heralds called Dublin and Cork.

In Europe, although coats-of-arms go back as far or further than in the United Kingdom, no institution similar to the College of Arms exists. However, in Germany, Austria, Belgium, the Netherlands, Norway, Sweden, and Spain there are various non-governmental offices which regulate the use of coats-of-arms.

A coat-of-arms consists of a shield bearing the heraldic device of the family. It can be divided into quarters and still further sub-divided to include the arms of families whose daughters married into the family. All these divisions are called quarterings, and there is one family in England whose shield bears no less than 356 quarterings—the Lloyds of Stockton-on-Cherbury, Salop.

You can obtain (or matriculate, as it is called) a coat-of-arms through any of the offices I have mentioned above. You will have to prove your direct descent from an arms-bearing family, be of good character and social standing, and have about $3,000 available. Or you can forget all the nonsense and concentrate your time and money on tracing back your ancestors—those men and women with no titles but of equal or greater nobility.

If you discover that you do have a legal right to a coat-of-arms, then feel free to decorate everything in sight with it. It is yours; you have the right to use it in any way you wish.

18 • Personal Stories

All of us who have traced our ancestors have stories to tell, and my wife and I are no exception. I will tell you some of our stories because the detective work involved in some of them may give you an idea to follow up in your own research. Even if you learn nothing of value, I hope you will capture some of the magic and romance of the journey on which you are now starting.

Earlier in the book (chapter 3) I told the story of when my wife and I were tracing her Pearson ancestors in Scotland and England. We had got back to 1710 when Christopher Pearson died in Sanquhar, Scotland, at the age of forty-one. Our problems arose because although his three sons were born in that town, there was no record of the birth of Christopher himself. The family story was that the Pearsons had originated in England. Perhaps this was the man who came from that country, but how could we find out?

We knew one important fact. In the death entry in the church register he was described as "overseer of the leadmines in Wanlockhead." This is a village which lies midway between Leadhills and Sanquhar. The lead mines used to be the main local industry, apart from farming.

We thought long and hard about his occupation. It would have been a skilled job that needed training and experience. He might have had a similar job in the place from which he came. So I wrote to the Ministry of Mines, in London, and asked if they could tell me where lead was mined in the north of England between 1689 and 1705. This covered the years from when he was twenty to the birth of his eldest son in Sanquhar. Basically, the enquiry covered the counties of Cumberland and Northumberland.

I soon heard back from the Ministry. They were most helpful and gave me a list of one hundred and fifty places where lead had been mined in that area and in that period. I had been expecting maybe twenty, but a hundred and fifty! However, we started writing to the local clergyman of each of the places mentioned, starting with those nearest to the Scottish border. (Remember, this was before the LDS International Genealogical Index was started.)

After negative replies from twenty of them, all telling us they could find no baptismal entry for Christopher in 1669, we said: "There must be an easier way than this!" Once again, we sat and meditated about the whole problem. Then my wife said, "Who owned the lead mines in Wanlockhead when Christopher was the overseer? Who owns them now? Perhaps there are records somewhere?"

This was a brilliant idea, and we started on this line of investigation and eventually found that the mines (which had been closed for seventy years) were owned by the Duke of Buccleuch. So I wrote to the Duke and explained our problem. He wrote back and said he was very sorry, but there were no records of the mines before 1814. In that year there had been a strike and a riot and the mine office had been set on fire and the records burnt.

That seemed to be that, but a couple of months later the Duke wrote to us again and said he had been thinking about us and our ancestor-hunt since my letter and his reply, and had now remembered there had been a Miners' Welfare Library, and he knew the books were in the custody of a Mrs. Weir, in

Leadhills, and perhaps there might be a book there which could be of help.

So, not long after this my wife and I paid a visit to Mrs. Weir —a very pleasant old lady. We told her about what we now called—in capital letters—THE PROBLEM. She said the books—some 200 of them—were stored in the attic, but she was sure there was nothing of any use. They were all religious books designed "to elevate the moral and spiritual tone of the miners." So there we were, back to square one!

Two months later Mrs. Weir wrote to us and said she had been looking through the books and had found one called *God's Treasure House of Scotland,* an account by a minister of visits he had paid in the middle of the last century to church-yards in the Sanquhar area. In it, he described the church there and its kirkyard and throughstones (these were horizontal tombstones which rested on four legs about eighteen inches above the grave). He wrote: "There is the resplendent tomb-stone of Christopher Pearson, overseer of the leadmines. The top of the throughstone, with a beautiful border of ivy leaves, bears this inscription:

> " 'Here lyes Christopher Pearson, overseer of the Lead Works in Wanlockhead. He was born at Bishopfield, in the parish of Allendale, in the County of Northumber-land, and dyed July 27th, 1710, aged 41.' "

This, of course, was the most wonderful stroke of luck—not only because it told us where Christopher came from, but also because the book described a tombstone which no longer exists. Many months before we had checked all the local graveyards, including Sanquhar. Somewhere about 1880 the road by the kirkyard had been widened and a number of tombstones had been moved and lost—including that of Christopher Pearson.

Our next move was to rush to our local library and look up the *Victoria County History* of Northumberland. We found the right volume for the Allendale area of the county, and looked up the index. There we found an entry which read:

"Pearson of the Spital, family tree," and also another entry: "Pearson, Christopher." We turned to the pages indicated and there we not only found the Pearson family tree taking us back to the fifteenth century, but also included in the tree was the entry of Christopher Pearson, born 1669. About him there was "No further information."

In other words, Christopher had left home and the local historians who had compiled the family tree did not know where he had gone. The Pearson family were the great land-owners of the district, Lords of the Manors of Haltwhistle and Allendale, owners of many farms, and owners of the local lead mines in Allendale. There were pages of information about the family, and references to other books which, in turn, gave us even more information about them. We wondered how Christopher had come to leave home and settle in Dumfriesshire, and we still wondered whom he married when he got there, but *at that time* we could not answer these questions.

We left Christopher in abeyance and again concentrated on going further back with the Pearson family. We were most successful, considering that we were working in a period prior to the very existence of church registers—in the area of manor-ial rolls, manor court leets, land taxes and records, pipe rolls, feet of fines, and so on. We eventually traced the family back to Wautier Pierssone, Count of Berwick, who was alive in 1296, and was mentioned in the Ragman's Roll as pledging allegiance to Edward I when he invaded Scotland.

Christopher was born at a farm called Bishopfield, in the parish of Allendale. He had two brothers and three sisters. One brother, William, died at the age of sixteen. The elder brother, Robert, inherited the farm from his father (also named Robert) in 1695. Christopher was twenty-six then and, presumably, looking after the family lead mines while his brother farmed. Both the sons were mentioned in the father's will:

> To my eldest son, Robert Pearson, five hundred pounds, and to my second son, Christopher, two hundred and fifty pounds.

To my eldest son, Robert, one bedstead, one table, one iron pot, and all my oxen gear with plows and harrows.

To my sons, Robert and Christopher, all the rest of the gear belonging the husbandry.

To my son Christopher one bedstead in the loft.

There were many other bequests to the daughters and the third son.

Christopher's brother married Catherine Fairless and died in 1753. The farm of Bishopfield was then bought by the Fairless family and today—over 200 years later—it is still owned and occupied by the family. Since the Pearsons built the farm in 1609 on land which they had owned since 1480, it means that in a period of over 500 years only the two families of Pearson and Fairless have owned the property—quite a record!

We went to Northumberland and met the Fairless family and we have kept in touch with them over the years. This led to a quite extraordinary event which I'll tell you about a little later on.

In digging into the Pearson family history in Northumberland we discovered a very colorful character—a first cousin of Christopher (and his brother Robert)—called William, who was born in 1670, a year after Christopher. William had a sister, Mary, who married a Matthew Leadbitter.

In 1715 an army crossed the border from Scotland, marching on London in an attempt to put the Stuarts back on the throne, specifically, James, the "Old Pretender," father of Bonnie Prince Charlie. The Earl of Derwentwater, the greatest landowner in the north and a cousin of the Old Pretender—and of William Pearson—raised a force of several hundred men in Northumberland to join the invading army. William joined him in the rebellion and became a colonel in the rebel forces. He took part in the Battle of Preston, in which the rebels were defeated, and was taken prisoner and nearly hanged. He escaped from his guard and some months later was arrested near his cousin Robert's house at Bishopfield. The other leaders were all executed, but Colonel Pearson was lucky. He was only fined, but it must have been a large sum because in that year he sold the Manor of Haltwhistle for £1,100, and the family home at Hexham, the Spital, for £1,325. This we found out, of course, from land records. He died six years later at the age of thirty-one.

We also found references in the local history books to an oil painting of William and thought how wonderful it would be if it was possible to trace it, if by any chance it still existed. We knew he had no children to inherit it; and then we thought of his sister, Mary, who had married Matthew Leadbitter. Could she have inherited the painting? If so, what had happened to the Leadbitter family in the last 230 years?

So we traced the Leadbitter family and found that the head of the family was Sir John Leadbitter, then the Clerk to the Privy Council in London. We wrote and asked him if, by chance, the portrait still existed. He replied and said, "Yes, my brother in Devonshire has it." We were thrilled, and off we went to Devon to see the painting. It showed William Pearson with long, fairish hair, wearing an apricot-colored velvet jacket, with lace at his neck and wrists. He was obviously a bold and strong character, and, strangely enough, bore a very great resemblance to my wife's father!

On the back of the portrait the following remarks were written by an uncle (born in 1835) of Sir John Leadbitter and his brother:

> My father (born 1787) I am sorry to say does not know much about Colonel Pearson. Our late Uncle Nicholas (born 1786) and Uncle Charlton were well up in these matters. From his recollection he was present at the Battle of Preston, on the Jacobite side, and his title was taken from his association with Charles Stuart's forces. At the aforesaid battle he was taken prisoner and nearly hanged. He was renowned as a very brave, resolute, and determined man. He once started to fight a duel

with swords with a man in a yard in London, and his
antagonist bolted over a wall and disappeared—not liking
the prospect.

That was the end of the Pearson story at that time, but
ancestor-hunting never really stops; one is always looking for
a few more bits of information. Over the years since then we
have filled in a few gaps:

(1) From the sasine registers in Scotland we found that
Christopher Pearson's widow was Margaret Cunningham. So
that finally told us whom he had married.

(2) From an old history of lead mining in Scotland we found
that the lead mines in Wanlockhead were leased in 1691 to a
Matthew Wilson of Allendale, Northumberland. The Wilsons
were connected by marriage to the Pearsons and also owned a
lead mine nearby, so that was the reason Christopher left home
and became overseer in Wanlockhead—probably in the year
when the mines were leased by his cousin Matthew Wilson, and
when he was twenty-two years old.

There was one more extraordinary event in our search for
the Pearson ancestors. A few years ago, when I was visiting
England on business, I went to lunch with the Fairless family at
Bishopfield. While I was there Mrs. Fairless said, "Last year,
we took down the old barn at the back of the house, and in the
rafters—in the high 'V' of the roof—we found a sliding panel
and a secret hiding place. In it were the remains of a straw
mattress, a couple of water bottles, and a pistol. We cleaned
the pistol up and sent it to the British Museum for identification. They told us it had markings on the barrel which showed
it had been issued to an army officer in the year 1715. Now,
how on earth could that have got there?"

I almost leapt out of my chair with excitement! "My God,"
I said, "I can give you a terrific guess! You know all about the
famous William Pearson who escaped after being taken prisoner
at Preston. As an officer he would have been guarded by an
officer. When he escaped he probably did so by knocking out

the guard, and quite naturally would have taken his pistol. Then he would have taken off for Bishopfield where he knew his cousin Robert would help him. The two lads would have built a hiding-place where William could go when the hunt for him got too close. On the particular day when we know he was caught, he must not have been keeping a good look-out."

"I think you are absolutely right," said Mrs. Fairless, holding out the pistol, "so here it is—take it back with you to Canada and give it to your wife. The Pearsons have a better right to it than the Fairless family."

So now we have it with us in Canada, a constant reminder to my wife of her brave and romantic ancestor, and an example to both of us of the magic and rich rewards of ancestor-hunting!

I did not find anything as exciting in my search for my Baxter ancestry, but I did have one extraordinary experience which has lived with me ever since. Many years ago, on a spring morning, just after daybreak, I was poking about in the ruins of an old farmhouse in Swindale. The silence was total and there was no living creature within ten miles of me, except for a few sheep grazing nearby—perhaps the tough Herdwicks bred by my ancestors for eight centuries. I found a massive beam which must have been the original support for the upper story. Suddenly, I noticed some faint carving in the wood on one side. I rubbed away at the dirt and grime and picked away at the indentations with an old squared nail lying beside the beam. Finally, I could decipher it—JB 𝔖𝔐 IB 1539.

I knew who they were! John Baxter and his wife, Isabel Wilkinson, and 1539 was the year of their marriage. I also knew that in that year John was nineteen and his wife was eighteen, and they had been given the farm as a wedding present by John's father. Standing in the ruins, in the silence and the stillness of that lonely, lovely valley of my ancestors, I could picture the two youngsters setting up house together—John carving the initials in the heavy beam and Isabel holding the chair on which he stood. The beam is gone now—taken away for firewood, I suppose—but I remember that moment in my life when all my ancestors seemed to crowd around me and all my searching for my roots was worthwhile.

I am sure that you, too, will enjoy similar moments of wonder and magic and excitement.

19 • A Family History

I am often asked the difference between a family tree and a family history. The answer is simple. A family tree shows your actual descent in a clear and easily understandable format. An example of this was given in chapter 15. A family history is an account of your family and your ancestral background set out in narrative form. It enables you to go into much greater detail about your ancestors and their surroundings over the centuries than does a family tree. The latter can, of course, take any one of several forms. The example I gave was concerned with your *direct* ancestral line. A variation of this would be to include all your living relatives. Some people are more concerned with finding all their existing cousins than they are with trying to trace back the family over several centuries. Which route you take is for you to decide. Most of the larger genealogical or family history societies have for sale a variety of forms and books for recording information to fit your own requirements.

There are no forms for recording a family history, and none are required. I think the simplest way to explain it is for me to set out below the earlier part of a "Baxter Family History" I wrote some years ago after I finished tracing back that side of my ancestral line. The information I include about the area from which my family came, the details of their lives over the years, the details of the sheep they raised, the food they ate, the clothes they wore, were all the result of research into the social history of the district. This is something that anyone can do by buying or borrowing books. It is, in fact, something you *should* do if you really want to know about the people who formed you; it will put leaves on the bare branches of the family tree. For me, it was not enough to trace my family back for six centuries. I was not content with dates of birth, marriage, and death, and I wanted to really get to know them as men and women, to find out how they lived so that I could get a clear picture in my mind of these men and women whose names appeared in my family tree. To paraphrase the famous prayer of Sir Francis Drake, "It is not the roots and the tree which yieldeth the true glory but rather the leaves which adorn the branches."

The Baxters of Swindale and Morecambe

Swindale is a remote dead-end valley, or dale, located in the old county of Westmorland, now part of Cumbria. It is west of Shap Fell and almost midway between the towns of Kendal and Penrith. The wild and mountainous country was first populated by the Beaker people from Yorkshire and Northumberland who settled in the dales in 2000 B.C. They were farmers who were followed in 300 B.C. by the Celts, another farming people from Ireland. Two centuries later the Brigantes moved into the area from the east, followed in 100 A.D. by the invading Romans from the south. The Romans built their hill forts and roads, fought frequently with invaders from the north, and finally departed in 410 A.D. The Cymry then moved in from the north (Cumberland is named after them), and in 600 A.D. the warlike Anglians from the eastern Kingdom of Northumbria occupied the area. The name Westmorland originated at this time when the district was called Westmaringaland —"the land of the western border"— by the Anglians.

In 850 A.D. the first Vikings appeared—coming not from the east but from Ireland. They came as refugees fleeing from attacks from other Viking bands in a civil war raging in that island. From 950 to 1032 Westmorland was part of Scotland. It reverted to England in 1032, but in 1066 (the year of the Norman Conquest of England) the Scots seized control for a few years. As a result of these many invasions and settlements the place names of Westmorland include Celtic, Scots, Roman, Saxon, Viking, and Norman words.

In 1092, according to the *Anglo-Saxon Chronicle,* "William II marched north to Carlisle with a large army, re-established the fortress and built the castle, garrisoning it with his own men, and afterwards returned to the south, and sent thither very many peasants with their wives and stock to dwell there to till the ground." Since the name BAECESTRE is Saxon for baker, the first of the family in Westmorland may well have been one of the Saxons settled there by the son of the Conqueror.

The first mention of a Baxter in the area was in 1195 when John le Bacastre owned land at Helton Flechan (between Bampton and Askham) at the foot of Swindale, and now known simply as Helton. This is an Anglian word meaning, originally, the farmstead by the hill. Just above Helton is a grove of trees still known as Baxter's Rash—another word of Anglian origin. There is no further mention of the family in local records—few of which exist, of course—until 1340 when John Baxter is on record as owning a carucate of land at Helton. (Under the feudal system a carucate was as much land as could be tilled with one plow and eight oxen in a year.)

A few years earlier, in 1303, a William le Bakester, "a free tenant," held half a carucate at Castlerigg, some ten miles to the northwest, and paid four pence per annum to the Manor of Derwentwater. This was part of the vast estates of the Radcliffe family (Earls of Derwentwater). Most land in Westmorland (separated from Cumberland in 1190, but reunited with it in 1974 under the name of Cumbria) was held by a tenure which, though not technically freehold, gave the occupier security of succession. The land was poor and the local economy depended on the rearing and grazing of cattle and sheep and the production of wool.

In 1362 John Baxter of Helton Flechan and his wife, Beatrice, were mentioned in the will of Sir Thomas Lengleys, when he left them forty sheep. From this date until the present day the family records are complete. Soon after, in 1366, Thomas Baxter was living at Cliburn, about seven miles northwest of Helton, and with him was Joan, widow of Walter Baxter. Of course, with an occupational surname, there is no certainty this family was connected with the one at Helton, although I think we may assume they were.

In 1469 the family had moved the few miles from Helton to Bampton, and by 1496 they had prospered from the raising of sheep and built Bampton Hall, in the center of their 167 acres of land. They were now well-to-do "statesmen" with other neighboring families such as the Lowthers, Curwens, and Gibsons.

At this point I should explain the origin of the term "statesmen" as it applied to yeoman farmers owning their own land in the Lake District of England. Originally they were free men, but after the Conquest they found themselves tenants of their new Norman lords. They kept far more of their independence than the unfortunate "villeins" in other counties who became serfs. This was because the farmers in the Lakeland dales held their land by Border tenure. They retained their land as their own in return for their promise of military service in repelling any Scots invasion. The Normans and their successors, constantly threatened from the north, continued this arrangement.

An attempt was made in 1605 to end Border tenure and transfer ownership of the land to King James I and the great lords. There was a trial in the courts and the decision was that the lands were "estates of inheritance," quite apart from the promise of Border service, and so the "estatesmen" (statesmen) came into existence. They were their own masters. Each farm was a separate, independent estate, and each family raised or made its own food and clothing. The fluctuations of the market and the economy did not affect them at all directly.

In Swindale it was a particularly idyllic existence. They prospered with the wool trade; they were not affected by the plagues of 1208, 1268, 1319, or of the Black Death of 1348; they were untroubled by the Scots border raids since the main thrusts of the attacks were to the east and west of the remote valley. The Scots came south to Penrith, and then either went by way of Mardale and Windermere, or via Shap and Kendal—either way they left Swindale quiet and peaceful in the middle!

For this reason the houses were not fortified as were more exposed ones: there is no evidence of any pele towers in the dale, whereas on the main invasion routes they abounded. Bampton Hall is built of the local slate, low to the ground, and of two stories. The house still stands and is much the same as it was when it was built five centuries ago.

Apparently, though the Baxters had no trouble with the Scots, they did have problems with their neighbors to the east— the Gibsons of Bampton Grange. On 1 May 1469 the two families signed a bond in which they agreed their dispute should be arbitrated by Sir Thomas Curwen and Thomas Sandford. Part of the document is missing and so the cause of the trouble is unknown. Probably it was a dispute over boundaries or grazing rights for the sheep.

Each statesman had his own area on the fells and crags for grazing and this was called a stint. The Herdwick sheep raised in the area were reputed to know their own stints and to observe the boundaries. Perhaps, in this case, the Baxters and the Gibsons were too trusting!

The Herdwick sheep which the Baxters bred were the toughest of all the hill breeds, braving the highest peaks in the depth of winter for the sake of some minor nibbling. The Baxter stints—both owned and rented—covered eighteen square miles of Mardale and Swindale Commons, and this area could support 1,500 sheep. In the spring the ewes were brought down for lambing. In June the shearing took place. There were ten clippers at work and each could shear ten sheep an hour. In November the ewes were brought down from the fells for mating. One tup, or ram, could serve fifty ewes. The tup was smeared with red smit, or grease paint, and if a ewe showed no sign of this then it was obvious she had not been mated, and she was set aside to have the job completed. The smit came in a variety of colors to establish ownership among the sheep farmers. The Baxter dye was red, the Gibsons green, and so on, and all the colors used were registered.

Between 1500 and 1600 the selling price of wool multiplied five times, but wages and production costs remained stable. The average sheep produced 1½ stone (21 lbs.) of wool. The selling price per stone was 5 shillings in 1600, 7 shillings in 1700, and 10 shillings in 1800. With a flock of 1,500 this represented a good income for the family. Once a year buyers from Ghent, in the Low Countries, would come over to Newcastle-upon-Tyne, rent pack-horses and then head over the hills to the Lake District to buy the wool from the farmers.

Westmorland had a dialect and a language all its own. A ram was a tup, a ewe a yow, a growing lamb a hogg, a two-year-old a twinter, and a gelded ram a wether. The farmers also had a system of counting of unknown origin: (1) Yan (2) Tan (3) Tethera (4) Methera (5) Pimp (6) Sethera (7) Lethera (8) Hovera (9) Dothera (10) Dick (11) Yan-a-dick (12) Tan-a-dick (13) Tethera-dick (14) Methera-dick (15) Bumfit (16) Yan-a-bumfit (17) Tan-a-bumfit (18) Tethera-bumfit (19) Methera-bumfit (20) Gigot.

There may have been a Baxter house at the extreme head of the valley before the family built Bampton Hall. There are the ruins of a two-story house there and experts have estimated the date of building as about 1400. It appears on old maps as High Swindale Head House, but so far no definite information can be obtained about it. It had a large floor area measuring sixty feet by forty feet and some outbuildings.

The John Baxter who built Bampton Hall married Elizabeth Lowther in 1450. She was the daughter of Sir Hugh, one of Henry V's knights at the Battle of Agincourt. Her mother was Margaret de Derwentwater. This marriage allied the Baxters with the two most powerful families in Cumbria. John Baxter's grandson—another John—cemented the alliance still more by marrying Mary Lowther, daughter of Sir John and Mary Curwen. John Baxter's brother, Henry, then married another Mary Curwen and the next most powerful family was linked by blood to the Baxters.

The next generation—John Baxter (1520-1594)—brought "brass" and not "class" into the family. John married Isabel Wilkinson, whose family had a small but prosperous ironworks at Pennybridge. The son of this marriage, William (1540-1606), married Janet Holm, daughter of another wealthy local family. He was part owner of coal mines near Whitehaven, and his land in Swindale now totalled over 1,200 acres—quite apart from the enormous fell area over which he had grazing rights.

The next generation saw a parting of the ways in the Baxter family. The Baxter-Holm marriage produced five sons and one daughter. The latter married Thomas Curwen and the five sons farmed the ancestral land. The eldest, John, lived at Bampton Hall, while the others had farms at Tailbert, Bomby, Swindale-foot, and Swindalehead. History does not record whether the son who farmed the latter was bothered by the Swindale Boggle. This was the ghost of a woman in flowing white robes who haunted the fells in that area. She was supposed to have been a woman who starved to death in a remote fell cottage.

In 1600 the youngest son, James, married Mabel, daughter and co-heir of Sir James Preston of Ackenthwaite, near the border with Lancashire. He farmed a large estate there for the rest of his life and died in 1677, aged 101—the first and, so far, the last centenarian in the Baxter family. He had three sons —Thomas, John, and Miles. Nothing further is known of the last two, but Thomas married Janet Long and had three sons and two daughters.

The eldest son, Richard (1646-1720), married Elizabeth, daughter of Thomas Gibson of Bampton Grange, his second cousin. The Baxter-Gibson feud of 1469 had probably ended when Janet Baxter of Bampton Hall married Thomas Gibson of Bampton Grange in 1592.

Meanwhile, back in Swindale, the family continued to prosper. In 1703 Thomas Baxter, then the leading man in the area, gave 300 acres as an endowment to finance the building of a school. The indenture reads:

> Thomas Baxter, in consideration of his great affection towards the inhabitants of Swindale, and to promote virtue and piety by learning and good discipline, grants a messuage of 260 acres 3 rods 33 perches at Wasdale Foot in his manor of Hardendale, and another 31 acres 2 rods 9 perches in the manor of Crosby Ravensworth, that the trustees may build a school-house on some part of my grounds at Bampton, and make convenient desks and seats, and maintain a well qualified person to teach the English and Latin tongues, etc.

The school was built near the chapel in Swindale, and over the next century and a half the school produced many graduates who went out into the world to become clergymen, lawyers, and architects. It was said in Westmorland at the time: "In Bampton they drive the plow in Latin and shear the sheep in Greek."

Seven years after the school was built Thomas provided a free library. He was obviously far ahead of his time; for a tiny village in a lost dale to have such facilities in 1710 was unique.

The Baxters were mentioned by Nicholson and Burn in their book *History and Antiquities of the Counties of Cumberland and Westmorland* in 1777: "This Mr. Baxter and his forefathers for time immemorial have been called Kings of Swindale, living as it were in another world, and having no one near them greater than themselves."

The family remained in Swindale until 1796 when the estates were sold to the Earl of Lonsdale. The dynasty of the Kings of Swindale came to an end. The Herdwick sheep are still on the fells but the only memorial to the proud Baxters is a short lane beside Bampton Hall still called "Baxters' Lane"— though no one living nearby knows why!

There is more to the family history, of course, bringing it down to the present day, but I think I have shown you enough to demonstrate what can be discovered about the life of your ancestors.

There is so much for you to find out, and so much information is available if you research carefully. If your ancestors were immigrants to this country and you discover the date, then by delving into the history of the place from which they came you can find out why they came. Why did they leave home to make a new life across the ocean? Was it civil war? Starvation? The plague? The answers are there waiting for you to discover.

I wondered why my own ancestors left Swindale in 1796. I discovered that the reason was a rather strange one. In the winter the family members—men, women, and children— would comb and card the wool, and with a handloom turn it into homespun cloth. Then in the spring they would sell it. This income made all the difference to a large family with limited income from the sheep (the selling price of wool had dropped considerably). The year 1796 saw the invention of the spinning jenny, and this led to the establishment of mills, where one worker could supervise the operation of twenty looms. There was no longer any market for homespun cloth; the younger family members went into the mills in Kendal and Lancaster, and only the older people were left on the farm. That is why the Baxters left the land and why I am not raising sheep in that lonely, lost valley of my ancestors!